John Walker

The Cow and Calf

a practical manual on the cow and calf in health and disease - with a description of different breeds of beasts, their milking capabilities, dairy work and an article on the baneful ergot parasite in grasses

John Walker

The Cow and Calf

a practical manual on the cow and calf in health and disease - with a description of different breeds of beasts, their milking capabilities, dairy work and an article on the baneful ergot parasite in grasses

ISBN/EAN: 9783337198343

Printed in Europe, USA, Canada, Australia, Japan

Cover: Foto ©Lupo / pixelio.de

More available books at **www.hansebooks.com**

PRICE EIGHTEENPENCE.

THE
Cow and Calf:

A PRACTICAL MANUAL

ON

THE COW AND CALF IN HEALTH AND DISEASE.

BY JOHN WALKER.

LONDON:
THOMAS C. JACK, 45 LUDGATE HILL.
EDINBURGH : GRANGE PUBLISHING WORKS.

PERKINS
AGRICULTURAL LIBRARY

UNIVERSITY COLLEGE
SOUTHAMPTON

JOHN LAMPITT,
Engineer & Millwright,

Manufacturer of Improved Traction Engines, Portable Engines, Horizontal Fixture Engines, Vertical Engines, Water Wheels and Turbines, Thrashing Machines, Straw and Hay Elevators, Saw Tables, Mortar Mills, Corn Grinding and Crushing Mills, Flour Dressing Machines, General Millwork and Machinery.

VULCAN FOUNDRY,
BANBURY, OXON.
Maker of Tucker's Patent Ensilage Stack Press.

GUARANTEED GRASS SEEDS.

JAMES HUNTER,
AGRICULTURAL SEED MERCHANT,
CHESTER,

Who originated and introduced into this country the system of selling Permanent Grass Seeds (and all other Farm seeds) by guarantee, has obtained large supplies of the best samples of the late harvest, and is now re-cleaning and preparing them for distribution. These Seeds are offered as follows :—

The PURITY of each kind is GUARANTEED.
The GENUINENESS of each kind is GUARANTEED.
The PERCENTAGE of GERMINATION of each kind is separately stated and GUARANTEED.

Notwithstanding the superior quality of the Seeds, they are offered at very moderate prices, and taking into account their guaranteed germination, purity, &c., will prove the best and by far the cheapest Seeds in the market.

The Annual Price List is published in February.

TERMS.—Five per cent. discount for cash. Free delivery to any Railway Station in the Kingdom.

All Seeds are supplied separately, and are offered and sold subject to the analysis of the Consulting Botanists to the Royal Agricultural Society of England and the Highland and Agricultural Society of Scotland.

THE BEST SHORT TREATISE ON GRASSES :

"Permanent Pasture Grasses and the Adulteration of their Seeds."

New and Revised Edition.   *Gratis on application.*

All interested in Laying down Land to Grass, and who would discourage the use of Spurious and Adulterated Grass Seeds, should procure a copy of this valuable work.

1885-6.
OAKSHOTT & CO.'S
SEED
WHEATS
BARLEYS
OATS
BEANS & PEAS

Oakshott & Co.'s Selected Cereals
Have been awarded the Gold Medal and First-Class Certificate,
CALCUTTA.

DIPLOMA OF HONOUR,
LONDON INTERNATIONAL EXHIBITION.

SPECIAL PRIZE, AMSTERDAM EXHIBITION.
And our Customers have been awarded PRIZES
ALL OVER THE COUNRTY.

Samples and Prices, with our Practical Work on Seed Corn, beautifully illustrated with Coloured Engravings, sent, post-free, on application to

E. G. Oakshott + Co. Seed Corn Growers and Merchants,

READING, BERKS.

BENNETT'S BERKELEY VALE
CALF MEAL.

THE CHEAPEST AND BEST MILK SUBSTITUTE IN THE MARKET.
REQUIRES NO BOILING.   PREVENTS SCOUR.

PRICE 21s. PER CWT. CARRIAGE PAID.

Read the following testimony of those who use it:—
From Mr PETER, *Steward to Lord Fitzhardinge.*

HAM, BERKELEY, *Sept. 12th, 1885.*

DEAR SIR,—I should feel obliged if you would kindly send on the 5 cwt. Calf Meal I ordered of you the other day. I am highly pleased with it. I find it a capital substitute for milk, a preventative of scour, and it keeps the animal healthy and growing at a much less cost than milk.—Yours truly, JAMES PETER.

BROOKLANDS, FALFIELD, *Oct. 6th, 1885.*

DEAR SIR,—Send me on another lot of Bennett's Calf Meal; the 6 cwt. I had of you is all gone—I cannot speak too highly of it. It is a good preventative of scour, and a very economical means of rearing Calves.—Yours truly, G. STRICKLAND.

Mr T. IND, *Yate.*

MANUFACTURED BY

JOHN BENNETT, Cam, Dursley, Gloucestershire.
AGENTS WANTED IN UNREPRESENTED DISTRICTS.

THE GADFLY OF THE OX
(*Œstrus Bovis*),

Their History, Life, Prevention, Destruction, and Losses Sustained thereby,

Computed at £2,474,195 Annually in Great Britain.

BY JOHN WALKER,
Author of "The Cow and Calf," "Wheat Mildew," "Ergot and its Abortive Influences," &c

PRICE SIXPENCE.

LONDON: THOMAS C. JACK, 45 LUDGATE HILL.
EDINBURGH: GRANGE PUBLISHING WORKS.

TOO LATE!

Is not a phrase merely reserved for great national misfortunes, but is more often applicable to our common lot and actions, and consequently the term is well understood when its force has been felt at home. How many have mourned a loss which they knew the exercise of a little forethought would have obviated? How many animals, even in our day, are annually lost for want of a little prudence on the part of their owner or tender? The healing art, like many other things, is not difficult if applied at the commencement or infancy of disease; and with a few well-proved medicines, the mastery over disease (humanly speaking) may be obtained, and the mournful "TOO LATE" never be heard. You ask for well-proved medicines. We rely on our universal good name, for nearly 50 years freely granted, to speak the volume in favour of

DAY & SONS' World-Renowned and Matchless HORSE & CATTLE MEDICINES.

THE "ORIGINAL" UNIVERSAL MEDICINE CHEST.
Price £2. 4s. 0d.
Carriage Paid.

And No. 11,

UNIVERSAL CHEST
Price £5. 0s. 0d.

Both Chests contain
DAY & SONS' GUIDE,
"*Everyday Farriery.*"

Awarded 24
GOLD & SILVER MEDALS.

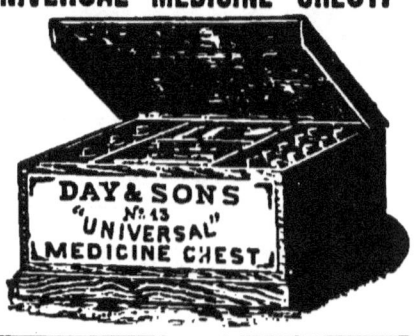

DAY & SONS' "UNIVERSAL" MEDICINE CHEST.
Price £2. 4s. 0d.; contains the following world-famed and matchless Preparations:—

		£	s	d
2 Bottles Purified Driffield Oils,	for Wounds, Kicks, Cuts, Bruises, &c.,	0	5	0
6 Bottles Black Drinks,	for Colic, Scour in Cattle, Blown, &c.,	0	10	0
8 Red Drinks,	for Cleansing after Calving, and Milk Fever,	0	8	0
1 Bottle White Oils,	for External Injuries, Weak or Swollen Joints,	0	2	6
1 Dozen Alterative Powders,	for Coughs, Colds, Sore Throats in Horses,	0	3	6
1 Dozen Ewe Drenches,	for Fevers, Colds, or Chills	0	3	6
1 Bottle Foot Rot Oils,	for Foot Rot in Sheep,	0	2	6
3 Bottles Husk Draughts,	for Husk or Hoose,	0	5	0
1 Can Aromatic Chalk Mixture,	for Diarrhœa or Scour,	0	2	6
1 Guide, "Everyday Farriery,"	giving Symptoms and Treatment,	0	1	6
		£2	4	0

N.B.—Any of the above Medicines may be had separate, securely packed in Wood Cases.

CAUTION! Beware of spurious but <u>apparently</u> clever imitations, and see you address all Orders to

CREWE, CHESHIRE.

REGISTERED. TRADE MARK.

PRIZE COW AND CALF.

THE SIRE OF THE HERD (EARL OF OXFORD),
Head of his Class at the Royal Show at Preston, and at many other Exhibitions.

THE COW AND CALF

A Practical Manual

ON

THE COW AND CALF IN HEALTH AND DISEASE

WITH A DESCRIPTION OF DIFFERENT BREEDS OF BEASTS
THEIR MILKING CAPABILITIES, DAIRY WORK

AND AN

Article on the Baneful Ergot Parasite in Grasses

BY

JOHN WALKER

AUTHOR OF "CATTLE POISONS," "WHEAT MILDEW," "THE GAD FLY
AND ITS DESTRUCTION," ETC. ETC.

Second Edition.

LONDON
THOMAS C. JACK, 45 LUDGATE HILL
EDINBURGH: GRANGE PUBLISHING WORKS
1887.

THE COW.—If civilised people were ever to lapse into the worship of animals, the cow would certainly be their chief goddess. What a fountain of blessings is the cow: she is the mother of beef, the source of butter, the original cause of cheese, to say nothing of shoe-horns, hair-combs, and upper leather. A gentle, amiable, ever-yielding creature, who has no joy in her family affairs which she does not share with man. We rob her of her children that we may rob her of her milk, and we only care for her when the robbing may be perpetrated."—*Household Words.*

PREFACE.

"All is the gift of industry; whate'er exalts, embellishes, and renders
life delightful."

HAVING consulted the almost inexhaustible literature of the agricultural library, we have found no book devoted to the *cow* and *calf* pure and simple. It is our present humble effort, then, to present such a small work as is capable of being utilised by every cow-keeper. As we have passed the time from youth to age among the animals of the farm, present counsel is given from actual experience, and he who has guided the plough, handled the scythe, sickle, and milkpail (being at the same time studiously inclined), is more competent to wield the pen than a semi-practical author. Even taking wisdom as our guide in these days of limitless competition from the foreigner, it is difficult to make the occupation of the soil remunerative; indeed, it is impossible to do so without, as occasion demands, passing from the old ruts to the newly-defined grooves of modern improvements.

Some little repetition, or rather tautology, may be observed in this manual, but trust it will be pardoned by our critics when it is understood that we desire each part of the work to appear complete in itself.

Our primary aim has been to thoroughly define each subject, and render it comprehensible alike to the amateur and also to the proficient agriculturist who needs little counsel. As elsewhere observed, *animals* of the farm must for the future support those whose daily bread depends upon the products of their land, for it is profitless to waste more time in the turning of the furrow. Historical record corroborates the fact, that the pasture lands of Britain have from distant ages been famed alike for their rich herbage and the unsurpassable quality of the bovine tribe that have fed upon them.

We trust the darker clouds are clearing from the farmer's horizon, and hat the faint glimmer of light, only just perceptible, may expand into a long succession of sunny seasons. Thus we set our little work, with canvas stretched, upon the somewhat troublous tide of public approval.

J. WALKER.

THE COW AND THE CALF.

INTRODUCTION.

YEAR by year it is becoming more clearly defined that Great Britain and Ireland must be converted more largely into pastoral countries. Wherever arable land is of such a quality as to lay kindly down in grasses, no delay should be made in so transforming it; for if agriculturists persist in competing with foreign nations in grain-growing, ruin will assail them as sure as night follows day—always providing that the husbandman is in no way protected. Freights are continually reduced, and in many instances large quantities of grain are brought over as ballast, free of cost. New corn-lands are being opened in many parts of the world. India has made large strides in this industry within the last few years, and may be looked upon as rapidly developing into a large corn-growing land.

Wars, and rumours of wars, may raise the price of wheat for short intervals; but such an uncertain chance of selling remuneratively will not keep the wolf from the farmer's door. Hostilities cannot endure for any lengthened period in the present day,

A

weapons of war being now so destructive that prolonged strife would result in total annihilation.

British corn-growing being, then (to any extent), a thing of the past, the plough must be cast aside, and the breeding, rearing, and fattening of cattle and sheep substituted. This occupation is the only bright star that illumines the farmer's horizon, and by this beacon he must direct his craft. ' The despondent grazier displays considerable alarm when he observes the immense cargoes of frozen mutton landed, sweet and good, from the other side of the globe; also the weekly imports of live cattle and quarters of beef by no means re-assure him. Howbeit, while the pasture-lands of England are well cared for she will rule the meat market. No country in the world can combine such rich pasture-land, suitable climatic influences, and valuable breeds of sheep and cattle as Great Britain. Neither can any other country boast of such intelligent breeders, and men who know better how to administer to the requirements of the cow herd or sheep flock.

Seeing, then, that breeding, rearing, dairying, and fattening must be the employment of the British farmer in future, the writer's purpose is, in the first instance, to point out the most remunerative cows for the different classes of dairy people to keep. This is a subject which has seldom been discussed through the press—more seldom in a clear, concise, and intelligible manner. Readers desirous of improving their knowledge with regard to the minute treatment of cattle have despaired of ever finding the manual that defines to the amateur in sufficiently simple terms the necessary information. Books are written by the gross, professing new doctrines, highly scientific experiments; but these do not meet the thousand and one little requirements of the inexperienced cattle-breeder.

"Pray, why is this?" my readers may inquire. Simply, because the majority of authors never obtained practical information with regard to the daily habits and needful treatment of cattle in health and disease. Small matters like these should particularly engage the farmer's attention. Every stock-owner should know how to treat simple diseases to which his cattle are subject, and be able to check any more intricate and malignant malady, until the qualified veterinary surgeon can be summoned to the spot.

The empiric should not be allowed amongst cattle under any pretext; for the grazier who is not capable of treating his animals more effectually than the quack, is not equal to hold the situation of stock-owner in these days of keen competition. Every farmer's son should receive an elementary education in this branch of his occupation when about to embark upon a pastoral farm. It will be seen that, where one case falls out that is really of so serious a character as to require the presence of a veterinary surgeon, twenty will yield to remedies which every qualified farmer can provide with the simple contents of a well-stocked medicine-chest.

In conclusion, the stock-master, however well versed he may already be in the treatment of animals, must remember that wide fields of knowledge still lie open for his future study and improvement; and while he is thus acquiring knowledge for himself, he is working "pro bono publico."

Different Breeds of Cows.

There are in Great Britain and its adjacent countries a variety of breeds of animals, far too many to comment upon here. The quaint, semi-wild Scotch kine, and others, on their native soil—

> "Hard, ragged, and rough as their heathery haunts,
> As the hills where they love to dwell,"

are only occasionally brought further south, to be fattened for the butcher on luxuriant pasture, under a more genial sky. Just over the Borders the productive little breed of Ayrshire thrive under the care of their "canny" masters.

The North and South Wales are reared for the most part in mountainous districts, where only scanty herbage prevails for them in summer and still harder fare in winter. Between the ages of eighteen months and three years old they are annually disposed of to the English graziers in large herds. Having fared hardly, and 'arrived at nearly full growth, they quickly make rapid improvement on the rich English pasture-land.

Ireland can boast of the far-famed Kerry cow, and some other kinds, most of them being, however, of a nondescript breed; but here and there the blood of good English shorthorns has made marked improvements in the herds. Then there are, among a variety of others, the shorthorn, the Hereford, the long-horned, and the Suffolk Dun. These latter kinds are indigenous to our country, and can be found on no other portion of the globe, bred, reared, and fattened to such perfection. Lastly, the Alderney, which will presently be fully spoken of under the heading of the "Gentleman's cow."

DIFFERENT BREEDS OF COWS.

The Scotch breeds do not, as a rule, yield large quantities of milk, although such as they do give is of excellent quality, and when more generously fed on English land, the cream is peculiarly rich in butter-forming constituents. In some districts it is a practice to introduce one or two Highland or Kyloe cows into the English dairies, in order to increase the richness of the milk of other cows, the produce of which may be remarkable rather for quantity than quality. The Ayrshire is essentially a dairy breed, and possesses such admirable qualities for the latter purpose as to be held in high esteem in districts other than those of Scotland.

The colour of the Ayrshire is for the most part red and white, in distinct patches; occasionally they are all of a red colour, more or less deep. We have sometimes seen the patches approach a fawn colour, and we have also seen prize Ayrshire bulls of a greyish colour. Red and white spotted may, however, be considered the standard marking of an Ayrshire. The horns are short, spreading a little at their junction with the head, and then turning upwards. Their other prominent points are a fine, tapering head, with pleasing countenance; thin neck; narrow chines, backs, and hocks; flat ribs, large belly, thin buttocks, fine bone, thin hair, and soft hide. Udder of a hemispherical shape, well formed, having loose, soft skin behind. The milk produced is rich in butter-making properties. A feature of the Ayrshire cow is the length of time over which its milk-producing powers extend. The following results of a milking competition at Ayr show the milking capabilities of this breed :—

Cow belonging to	1st Milking Friday Morning	2d Milking Friday Night	3d Milking Saturday Morning	4th Milking Saturday Night	Total Quantity of Milk	Average	Amount of Butter Produced	Time Occupied in Churning
	lbs. oz.	lbs. oz.	lbs. oz.	lbs. oz.	lbs. oz.	lbs. oz.	lbs. oz.	hs. min.
1. A. Wilson, Carrick St., Ayr.	22 14	21 14	27 12	24 6	96 14	24 3.5	3 4	0 25
2. James Hendrie, Balston, Ayr.	22 5	24 11	26 0	24 4	97 4	24 5	2 14½	0 50
3. W. Reid, Clune, St. Quivox.	23 0	25 7	11 3	22 9	82 3	20 8.75	2 9	0 45
4. W. Reid, Clune, St. Quivox.	30 15	25 12	24 12	27 15	109 6	27 5.5	3 6½	1 45
5. R. Wallace, Kirklandholm, do.	28 11	28 6	28 14	28 3	114 2	28 8.5	1 9½	2 5
6. R. Wallace, Kirklandholm, do.	25 5	23 13	23 9	22 0	94 11	23 10.2	1 15	1 45

The North and South Wales are a hardy breed, supplying to our markets some of the best beef on offer. They are good, fair milkers, and when crossed with the shorthorns are hard to rival. They will not, however, answer for the breeder and rearer to utilise, as their progeny would not be as valuable as something nearer approaching the shorthorn. A cross between a shorthorn and Welsh must not, however, be depreciated. Steers of this mixture have ere now proved good enough to compete successfully in the showyard; indeed, as a rule, they are splendid fleshed animals, hardy in constitution and apt at fattening. Howbeit, the writer has reared them side by side with well-bred, or rather nearly pure, shorthorns, and the latter have ever proved the most valuable animals in the end. For the first eighteen months the Welsh will hold their own, but during the next year or two a marked difference is observed. Again, there is still another drawback, viz., after the first cross the progeny are not so much to be depended upon. This experienced men find to be the case in crossing pretty well all animals. The first movement is a success; but later on all kind of nondescript creatures turn up.

The Kerry is a large yielder of milk, and a remarkably useful little cow, as light-hearted as its countrymen. It is to be regretted that up to the last few years it has been much neglected; but in these days of pastoral farming it is again sought out and found to be remunerative. This cow is hardy in constitution and active in habits. The head is small, fine, and furnished with bright intelligent eyes; the horns are short, and turn upwards. The carcase is round and rather long, the legs are short. The hindquarters are light, but high-boned, and wide over the hips. The colour is of a varied description, sometimes black, sometimes brindled, sometimes of a greyish mixture, and occasionally mingled with all these shades.

English Breeds of Cows.

The shorthorned or Durham stands out far in advance of any other kind. It is the breed *par excellence* of Great Britain, although now distributed over many parts of the globe. It is distinguished by its own excellences, the facility with which it communicates these to the animals of other breeds, and by its remarkable adaptability to the various circumstances of soil and locality. A lady writing upon this excellent breed of animals a few years ago, observed: "These shorthorns have such an aptitude to lay on flesh that they will get fat while many other breeds are thinking of it." Indeed, the writer himself has many times marvelled at the short interval it takes for cows or heifers of this description to get fat upon some really rich pasture-land. They usually arrive at a ripe state before the steer and bullock; but in Lincolnshire, and one or two other favoured spots in England, the first lot of large oxen can be got off from pasture in June, and the next lot before the entry of winter.

One drawback, however, attends these otherwise faultless cows, and that is, they are not, as a rule, good milkers. Many lovers of the shorthorned try to disbelieve this; but years of experience have taught the writer that just as a shorthorn will go round a lower breed in fattening, so will many a three-cornered cross-bred animal, rejoicing in perhaps many mixtures of blood, put the Durham out of sight in milk and butter productions. The milk of the latter is only of moderate quantity, and the quality varies very much, while it is seldom that they hold up the supply for an extended period. We have had an abundant supply of milk for three months, and suddenly the quantity has been reduced to half, and shortly from half to none. Others supply for a more extended period, but few longer than seven or eight months. Nevertheless it is found, as a rule, that where these animals are not too highly fed, and forced out of their natural healthy state, they are more capable of imparting very fair dairy qualities to their progeny. Our judges in the cattle showyards are now doing wisely by encouraging, in all ways possible, more natural and healthy-fed animals to compete for prizes. Another point in these animals' favour—and it is an important one—is the readiness with which they may be fattened for the butcher, after being used for

ENGLISH BREEDS OF COWS.

the dairy. The colour of the true-bred short-horn is either dark red or white, mixed red and white, or roan; any admixture of black is fatal to its pretensions—roan, however, may be said to be the favourite colour. As regards the points of merit of a shorthorned cow, the following are the ideas of the writer, and will doubtless compare favourably with the prominent features of many of our prize-takers in the showyard:—

	Number of Points.	What Constitutes Goodness.
Head	4	Moderate length, wide, and rather disked, with yellowish horns and flesh-coloured nose—not black.
Neck	1	Being well sprung from shoulders and slightly arched.
Neck-vein	2	Prominent and full.
Shoulder and crops	6	Former being well thrown back and wide at top, points well covered, and not prominent, crops being very full.
Breast	2	Coming well forward, wide and full.
Back	2	Breadth and levelness.
Loin	3	Breadth, and being well covered, not low.
Hocks	2	Breadth, and being at right angles with backbone.
Rumps	2	Not being drooped.
Quarter	2	Length, levelness, and being well filled up.
Thigh	2	Length and fineness, and being well beefed inwards.
Twists	3	Coming well down.
Hock	1	Being well bent, and not turned in.
Flank	3	Full, and coming well forward.
Back-ribs	3	Well sprung from back and round.
Fore-ribs	3	Round, and coming well down.
Quality and hair	4	Skin not being too thin, but soft and mellow, hair long and silky.
Colour	1	Roans and reds.
Udder and milk vessels	3	Well-formed teats and udders, large milk-veins.

The Hereford breed are a noble class, surpassed only in value as feeders by the Durham. Much of the richest pasture-land in England is yearly stocked with the pure Herefords, and they hold their own with any other large breed in our metropolitan markets. They grow to great size, and are usually given a year or two extra time to develop in over the shorthorns. Indeed up till recently (and even now in a few isolated instances), they were used for drawing the plough, and were not sold off for fattening until six or seven years old. Oxen of such an age are now few and far between, and are much sought after by wealthy graziers in the rich midland counties, and being got up for Christmas markets, are pictures worthy of observance.

Like the shorthorns, the Hereford cows have a failing, and it is in their milk-production. They are even in this respect less remunerative than the former, and are much used in their native county for calf-rearing. Hence it will be seen that the Hereford calf, being thus reared by the mother, has a really good start in the world, a great matter with all young animals on the farm. We do not purpose here to go into very minute particulars of this breed, for it is not likely intermixture of this blood will be needed to produce any of the dairy cows that will come under our notice in the present small volume.

Like the shorthorn, and some other breeds, the Hereford of to-day is a much nobler animal than it was a few decades ago; and their native county breeders may be well proud of their favourite. Foreign breeders are not so partial to it as the "Durham"—perhaps from its inadaptability to various climates.

The colours in the Herefords are a rich red on the body, and a clear white on the face, throat, belly, the lower part of the legs, and the tip of the tail. The forehead is broad, the hide thick, but mellow, the hair soft, and sometimes curly. The oxen are very heavy, and much larger in proportion than the cows. The flesh is excellent, and the animals are easily fattened. Although, as before observed, they are not a dairy breed, we have seen cows which were heavy milkers, and doubtless the attention which has been paid to the development of the grazing properties of the breed has destroyed whatever qualifications it may have possessed at one time for the dairy. George Culley, who wrote in 1801, says, on the authority of Mr. Ellman, referring to the Hereford cattle of that day—" The calves run with the cows till they are eleven or twelve weeks old, when they are weaned and turned to grass. A good cow, after the calf is taken from her (if well kept), will produce from 6 to 8 lbs. of butter a week for three or four months after taking off the calf, and double that quantity of skimmed-milk cheese. They do not give so large a quantity of milk as the Suffolk cattle, but it is much richer in quality." The above quantity of butter is liberal for any cow to make after rearing a calf, and it may be taken for granted that such a yield seldom occurs from the Hereford. Perhaps a cow may sometimes be slightly crossed with a good milk-producing kind; or one that is fed beyond the common might milk freely; but it must not be expected, and will scarcely occur in a breeder's herd in a lifetime. So it will be seen, while the Herefords reach within measurable distance of the top of the bovine standard in meat-producing qualities, it is by no means a remunerative milker.

The *longhorns* are fast passing away, and are readily discernible from all other breeds by the disproportionate length and sometimes encumbering forms of their horns. In the old Craven breed, the horns projected almost horizontally; but in the offspring and improved varieties, they either grew perpendicularly down, so as to render grazing difficult, or made such curvatures as to threaten to meet before the muzzle, or swept so round as to threaten to lock the under jaw, or turned their points so inward upon the nose or other parts of the face as to seem to be about to pierce them. Most of the present English longhorns have long, spreading, and sometimes drooping horns; a dark red and brindled colour, with white along the back; good coats of hair; rather coarse bones; fair symmetry; a good adjustment of beef along the back; a capacity of attaining great weight; and a habit of both sound and somewhat rapid feeding. But even the Craven group, like the whole of the Irish longhorns, though with no such wide difference of value, are divisible into two great and very distinct sections. The smaller Cravens inhabit the moorlands and hills, are hardy and easily kept, yield a large produce of excellent milk, have a capacity of rapid fattening when removed to good pastures, are much and justly prized by cottiers and small farmers. The larger Cravens inhabit the low and level districts, and yield less milk, in proportion to their size and food, than the smaller Cravens, but possess an extraordinary tendency to fatten rapidly, and to acquire a great bulk and weight. "As either of these found their way to other districts," remarks Mr. Youatt, "they mingled to a greater or less degree with the native cattle, or they felt the influence of change of climate and soil, and gradually adapted themselves to their new situation, and each assumed a peculiarity of form which characterised it as belonging to a certain district, and rendered it valuable and almost perfect there. The Cheshire, the Derbyshire, the Nottinghamshire, the Staffordshire, the Oxfordshire, and the Wiltshire cattle were all essentially longhorns, but each had its distinguishing feature, which seemed best to fit it for its situation, and the purposes for which it was bred. Having assumed a decided character, varying only with peculiar local circumstances, the old longhorns, like the Devons, the Herefords, and the Scotch, continued nearly the same." The longhorns were cherished in preference to all other breeds, and maintained to be the best by the celebrated improver, Mr. Bakewell; but they are generally admitted now to be decidedly inferior in aggregate worth to the shorthorns, and not equal for the shambles to any one of several of the Scotch breeds.

The writer saw some bullocks and heifers being got up for last Christmas market, crossed from the longhorns and Herefords, that showed good size, excellent quality, and extraordinary aptitude for fattening. They scarcely, however, as a pure breed meet with the requirements of the present day, and will quite likely become shortly an extinct race.

The Suffolk Dun or the Suffolk cow is the last species we can find space to treat upon here. It is a good all-round milker, being proved by the dairymaid alike for making good cheese, high quality of butter, and giving rich milk. It is the only true hornless breed in England, and is supposed to have originated from the polled or hornless breeds of Scotland. The colours generally met with are a light dun or yellowish cream, light red or red and white. The carcase generally is rather narrow and flat, legs short and thin, ribs well arched, belly heavy, chine thin and hollow, loin narrow. The head is fine, throat clean, dewlap not large. The udder is large and square, the milk veins large. The skin is fine, the hair silky. The general appearance of the Suffolk is bony or angular, not presenting the fine rounded outlines of the shorthorn, the Devon, or the Hereford. It is an animal, when dried off, capable of being quickly fattened up for the butcher when generously fed, and might, we think, taking it all in all, be more widely utilised in our dairies, either as a distinct breed or for crossing purposes.

The Gentleman's Cow.

It may not be at first quite apparent to my readers why certain cows are more suited to hold different positions; later on, however, it will be shown that while the "Alderney" is most at home in the nobleman's paddock or park, a different class is called for on the tenant-farmer's holdings. Again, between the rearer, or what we will in the future deem breeder, and the seller of milk, other varieties still are needed.

Alderney.

Sir George London

WORKS ISSUED BY SUTTON & SONS, READING.

PERMANENT PASTURES.
REPRINTED from the JOURNAL of the ROYAL AGRICULTURAL SOCIETY of ENGLAND,
By MARTIN H. SUTTON, M.R.A.S., F.R.H.S., &c.
PUBLISHERS: HAMILTON, ADAMS & CO., 32, PATERNOSTER ROW, LONDON.

SUTTON'S FARMER'S YEAR-BOOK & GRAZIER'S MANUAL.
PUBLISHED ANNUALLY IN FEBRUARY.

SUTTON'S AMATEUR'S GUIDE IN HORTICULTURE.
PUBLISHED ON JANUARY 1st, PRICE 1/- POST FREE. GRATIS TO CUSTOMERS.

SUTTON'S AUTUMN CATALOGUE of Bulbous Flower Roots, &c.
PUBLISHED ANNUALLY IN AUGUST.

THE CULTURE OF VEGETABLES AND FLOWERS,
FROM SEEDS & ROOTS, BY SUTTON & SONS, READING.
THROUGH ALL BOOKSELLERS.
From HAMILTON, ADAMS & Co. 32, Paternoster Row; or direct from SUTTON & SONS, post free for 5s.

MEDALS &c.

Nice, 1884.

Manch., L'pool & N. Lan. Agrl. Society, 1882 and 1883.

Cape of Good Hope, 1882.

Royal Hort. Soc., Knightian, 1881.

Melbourne, 1880.

Paris, 1878, 5 Medals.

Vienna, 1873.

Highland, 1872.

Paris, 1867, 2 Medals.

Odense, 1863.

Royal Berks Hort. Soc.

"The 100 acres of Permanent Grass Seeds were sown this spring, and came up well."—Court Knuth De Knuthenberg. Chamberlain to H.M. the King of Denmark.

"We have a capital plant on the 100 acres of Grass Seed supplied by you."—Mr. Jno. Campbell, Bailiff to the Rt. Hon. Lord Pitt Rivers, Rushmore.

"During a long course of experience I have never had or seen better Grass Seeds. They have made an excellent mark."—C. B. Edwardes, Esq., Peterborough.

"The (Grass) Seeds have been tested and come out very satisfactorily."—W. J. Malden, Esq., R.A.S. Experimental Farm, near Woburn.

"Major Sergison said he had sent the seed (70 acres) which he had purchased of Messrs. Sutton and Sons of Reading, to Professor Carruthers for analysis, and had received a most satisfactory reply."—Mid-Sussex Times.

"I suppose I am one of your oldest customers, and during those many years I have always had the most perfect confidence and satisfaction."—W. Porter, Esq., Hembury Fort.

"I sowed down a lot of land with your Grass Seeds many years ago which are clean and beautiful to this day."—B. Cail, Esq., Maidenhead.

MEDALS &c.

Amsterdam, 1883.

Royal Hort. Soc., Banksian, 1882.

Canterbury, 1882.

Brighton, 1881.

Royal Hort. Soc., Banksian, 1879.

Buenos Ayres, 1877.

London, 1873.

Norfolk, 1872.

Cape of Good Hope, 1865.

R. H. International, 1882, 6 Medals.

Royal Hort. Society's Linnæan

 SUTTON & SONS have no Agents for the sale of Seeds in the United Kingdom.

SUTTON & SONS, SEED GROWERS & MERCHANTS, Reading.
By SPECIAL WARRANT to H.R.H. the Prince of Wales.

The gentleman's cow is required to find milk, cream, and butter for the owner's household; cheese-making is seldom touched upon here. It is essential that the milk, cream, and butter should be of irreproachable quality, quantity not being taken so much into consideration. A warm cowshed and generous treatment is usually provided, therefore such animals live in happiness here that would waste into " screws " in more exposed quarters.

Again, rich men's dwellings are seldom situated in unfertile quarters, therefore nutrition and luxuriant herbage can be obtained in summer time, this being highly advantageous to a cow required to produce milk of the best quality.

Of every breed in the world none is more suitable to this position than the Channel Island cow, commonly called the "Alderney." Small, lean, and ill-favoured as it is, it nevertheless produces a higher class of milk than any other of the bovine species.

The beautiful yellow imparted to the butter cannot be obtained from any other source, while the cream is almost too thick to be termed a fluid. Even the breeder who desires to rear high-class animals is often induced by the dairy-wife to keep *just one* " Alderney " in his herd to give a better colour to the butter. Under the most generous treatment this cow carries comparatively little flesh, and is about as bad an animal to prepare for the butcher as can be found. Coming from a warmer climate than most parts of Britain, it requires careful attention in winter, and with such favour amply repays its opulent owner. It is of a gentle disposition, and when not abused by an unkind herdsman, seldom displays any vicious habits. One disadvantage is, that it is more liable to suffer from parturient apoplexy (dropping after calving) than any other sort.

Directions for treatment and prevention of this deadly disease will receive attention later on.

M. Le Cornu, writing in the Journal of the Royal Agricultural Society sometime since, considered the following points of merit to be regarded in a high-class Alderney:—1. Pedigree on the male side. 2. Pedigree on the female side. 3. Head small, fine, and tapering. 4. Cheek small. 5. Throat clean. 6. Muzzle fine and encircled with a light colour. 7. Nostrils high and open. 8. Horns smooth, crumpled, not too thick at the base, and tapering, tipped with black. 9. Ears small and thin. 10. Ears of a deep orange colour within. 11. Eye full and placid. 12. Neck straight, fine, and lightly placed on the shoulders. 13. Chest broad and deep. 14. Barrel-hooped, broad and deep. 15. Well-ribbed home, having but little space between the last rib and the hip. 16. Back straight from the withers to the top of the hip. 17. Back straight from the top of the hips to the setting on of the tail, and the tail at right angles with the back. 18. Tail fine. 19. Tail hanging down to hocks. 20. Hide thin and movable, but not too loose. 21. Hide covered with fine soft hair. 22. Hide of a good colour. 23. Fore-legs short, straight, and fine. 24. Fore-arm swelling and full above the knee, and fine below it. 25. Hindquarters, from the hock to the point of the rump, long and well filled up. 26. Hind-legs squarely placed, not too close together when viewed from behind. 27. Hind-legs not to cross when walking. 28. Hoofs small. 29.

Udder full in form, *i.e.*, well in line with the belly. 30. Udder well up behind. 31. Teats longish and squarely placed, being wide apart. 32. Milk veins very prominent. 33. Growth. 34. General appearance. 35. Condition.

The above would be the beau ideal of an "Alderney," and some of the points would be difficult to find. Within the last few years this breed has come very much more into favour, and in some instances has been crossed with other kinds to advantage. The dairy cow proper may be looked for in a cross between a shorthorn and "Alderney," indeed for a small farmer a mixture between the latter and an Ayrshire is valued. Too abrupt crosses, however, have not favour with the writer as a rule; for nondescript progeny may result. A step is just now taken in the right direction in the shape of a pure herd book entitled the "English Guernsey Cattle Society's Herd Book," the first volume being issued in 1885, and this will be likely to lead to an improvement in the breed.

The colour of these cows varies, but is usually of a faint yellow shade, mixed sometimes with white, and sometimes white and dun. The hair is short, and the warm winter garment provided for most other cows is not vouchsafed to the "Alderney." Thus it is necessary to provide the animal with comfortable winter quarters.

In addition to large imports from the Channel Islands, and occasional shipments from Normandy and the adjacent ports of France, large quantities are now annually bred in the more genial districts in England.

There are, and always will be, certain classes (not stock-owners by occupation) who feel pleasure in keeping one or two cows. For instance, the clergyman with his glebe, the opulent county gentleman, and the wealthy retired tradesman, have almost without exception a pet milk-supplier.

To such individuals among others this work is addressed. Every one who lives in the country should be able to use the advantages he possesses, and thus vie with his city neighbours. Prominent among rural privileges are the products of the dairy, the home-fed lamb or mutton, and the new-laid egg with the milk of freshness in its shell—which latter quality we might say is seldom or never found upon the citizen's table.

To those then who are blessed with plenteousness, and who reside in any but the most exposed localities in Britain, I can advise the Alderney cows as being most suited to their purpose. For it has been shown that their milk is most highly esteemed, the cream is of such consistency as to bear the proverbial mouse, *and the butter is second to none.*

The Breeder's Cow.

In choosing a herd of cows to breed and rear from, the young stock-master needs to use great care and foresight. It is not so much required that every animal should have reached a high state of perfection at the onset, as that cows should be bought that will in future improve into a valuable herd.

Short Horn.

The ordinary grazier cannot afford to go in for pure blood. It would be too expensive, and the attention, accommodation, and general requisites for a pure-bred herd are not to be found upon an ordinary farm, yet unless every appliance and means are at hand, it is unwise to start a pure-bred herd with a view of making profit. Indeed, the majority who have everything at their disposal often find the balance-sheet on the wrong side at their banker's, therefore it will be clearly seen that the common stock-master had better refrain from spending money on too high class and fancy stock; but at the same time he must bear in mind that inferior animals should not find their place on the breeder's establishment. It is well for stock-keepers generally that certain opulent people keep good pure breeds. They are the greatest boon to those who desire mixtures of blood, for in making crosses a pure strain should be procured either through sire or dam. What the breeder really requires to commence with are some nice breedy-looking heifers, such as would be perhaps three-fourths bred short-horns. A good age to buy them in at is two years old, and in choosing the sort, clear judgment is required—such judgment that the stock-keeper can only get by years of experience. Another time to lay in a stock is at three years old, this being the proper time for them to bring their first calves. Some farmers believe in breeding from heifers at an earlier date, either from two years or two years and a half old, but while the milking qualities of an animal are improved by this early breeding, the general size, symmetry, and constitution are deteriorated. It was for some time doubted if early breeding did really give a greater tendency for free milking, but practical and experienced men have now decided that such is the case.

It is, however, the object of the breeder to produce a good herd of beasts, that he may breed and rear from such animals that will meet a ready sale at any age. He may keep or sell the males, and use the heifers for the dairy, or he may keep both steers and heifers to go off when at maturity.

The object must be to breed steers that possess an aptitude for fatting, and heifers with a compact frame, gay carriage, and approved colours, so well appreciated by judges of high-class cattle. There is far more character needed in the head of a dairy cow than the inexperienced farmer dreams of in his philosophy. It should be carried with a jaunty air, and should be rather small than otherwise; not too short, but by no means long and thin, and not too far from the eye to the nostrils. The latter should expand, the forehead should be tolerably wide, while the eye should be large, full, soft, and expressive. There is something peculiarly interesting in the expression of a well-bred cow that will always be found wanting in one descending from questionable parents.

The horns should have that stout, mellow appearance that denotes a strong constitution and perfect health. In buying in a herd, colours will of course vary; but they should only be divided between deep reds, roans, and clear reds and whites, with flesh-coloured nostrils. White animals will turn up in a course of breeding, for it is a colour natural to the Durham breed, but not one to be encouraged. Indeed, in selling off an ordinary heifer down calving at three years old, a white animal would not make so much by at least a pound; neither are white steers admired for fatting purposes.

The Bag or Udder is particularly to be examined. A fortnight before calving it will have become so developed that a good judge should make no mistake. The teats should hang square; should be rather long and slender than thick and short. The slender teats denote good milking qualities in the cow, while thick short ones point to the reverse. Moreover, when they are so short, it is a most tedious process to milk the animals until they have had several calves. The result often is that such cows go dry first, this state often being brought about by the milker's neglecting to clean out the bag, being desirous of dispensing with an animal that gives them so much trouble. The bag needs not to be too big; it should, however, extend well up the twist. The udder is formed by the assemblage of the glands which secrete the milk, by the cellular tissue, fatty matter, ganglion, and by the outer skin or bag which envelops the whole. The milky glands are four in number, two on each side, and the whole constitute what are called the "quarters," so that each gland in a well-proportioned udder is about the fourth part of it. And here it is necessary to add that it is of great importance to see that all the quarters are perfect. It is a vulgar error to suppose that the udder is like a single bag or vessel, the contents of which may be withdrawn by any one of the teats. The very opposite is the fact; each quarter is separate from its neighbour, distinct by itself, so that if any one of the quarters is deficient—as is sometimes the case in practice—it simply amounts to a loss of so much of the milking qualities of the cow. In the majority of cows the supply of milk is in proportion to the size of the mammelles or milky glands. The following signs are indicative of a good constitution of glands:—(1.) Large development of the hind quarter; (2.) Lumbar region wide and strong; (3.) Rump extended; (4.) Large space to contain the udder gained by width apart of hind legs and haunches; (5.) Mammelles well developed, giving considerable size to the udder. It is necessary, however, to pay close attention to the structure of the udder, for it may be large, and yet the yield of milk may be small. The bulk of it should be made up of the milky glands, so that when the cow has been milked these shrink in dimensions, so that the udder, from a state of tension, becomes shrivelled up in creases or folds, soft and flabby. A fat or greasy udder, which does not yield much milk, remains almost of the same size after milking as before; it resists applied pressure, so that squeezing scarcely lessens it, its texture being uniform and firm. An udder of this sort is called fleshy. While, therefore, the udder should be large, it should not be fleshy, or rather greasy. Dealers, to prove to their customers that the udder is not greasy, draw back its outer covering or skin, and if it stretches much it is considered to be a good skin. It is easy to understand that skin which has been habitually distended and relaxed by great quantities of milk and its withdrawal, is sure to be more capable of being stretched than that which has not been subjected to such influences. Dealers have another object in view while thus extending the skin of the udder, namely, to prove that the cows have a fine, pliable, and soft skin. But inasmuch as the skin of the udder of all cows has these properties, it is necessary to go elsewhere—to the skin of the barrel or ribs—to prove the touch of the animal. The form of the udder is considered by some to be of great importance; some deem the udder best shaped when it is extended well forward, and the glands clearing in close contact to the belly. We have seldom found very good cows in which the udder has been shaped like a bottle hanging well downwards. Contrary to popular notions, the number of teats attached to the udder is six; four only are large and well developed, the other two being very small and placed behind, and seldom giving milk. The four large ones are those only to which attention is necessary. Their size depends upon the length of time which the cows have been milked or suckled by the calf; cows, therefore, which give much milk have large teats, because they are milked frequently and for a lengthened period. In this way only their size indicates the yield of milk. Usually more milk is obtained from the two back or hinder than from the two forward or front teats, and this because the hind-quarters of the udder are larger than the fore-quarters. The teats should be soft and flexible, not obstructed in their passage; and smooth, not indurated or shrivelled, on their surface. Warts are often present; but although they do not affect the milking capabilities of the cow, still they are better absent, inasmuch as they may be painful when touched, and thus cause the cow to be restless when being milked. Frequently they wear away from the friction of the hand after the cow has been milked for a short period. The position of the teats indicates the size of the glands. If they are huddled closely together, as each teat is connected with its own quarter, it follows that the quarters must be also closely together, and that the milky glands cannot be extensive. The teats, therefore, should be placed, as before observed, well apart from each other. But the form, nevertheless, of the udder exercises an influence on the position of the teats. Cows which have been long unmilked have the udder much extended, hard, and painful. Dealers, to convey the notion that bad cows are good milkers, endeavour to bring about this full appearance of the udder, and to effect it do not hesitate to carry out cruel plans. If the udder is hard, and much distended in proportion to its real size. If the teats are hard, wide apart, painful when touched; or if milk is seen to exude from them, even when untouched, it may at once be decided that the poor cow has been long unmilked.

Milk Veins.—The best signs indicative of a good milk cow are those afforded by the blood-vessels. If those surrounding the udder are large, bend in their course, and are varicose—that is, are not of uniform diameter throughout their length—they indicate that the glands receive much blood, are in full activity, and therefore that the milk will be abundant.

The veins on the stomach, or what are called the milk veins *par excellence*, are very easily observed, and are acknowledged by nearly all authorities to afford one of the best indications of the milking qualities of the cow. The milk veins issue from the udder in front and at the exterior angle, and in good cows form at this point a varicose swelling or dilation. Proceeding towards the fore-quarters, they form angles more or less marked, frequently dividing towards their hinder extremity, and finally disappear into the body by several openings. By compressing the milk veins at the points where they disappear into the body, we can make them dilate, and their size then can be well ascertained. The openings through which the milk veins disappear into the body are termed the milk ways (*portes du lait*) or fountains; but improperly so, for the blood contained in the veins which traverse them, in place of going to is returning from the glands, so that it is that portion which has not been utilised in the formation of milk, and may be termed the residue of the secretion. When the cow is not giving milk, the milk veins, from being little swollen, are not in proportion to or in accordance with (*en rapport*) its milking qualities. Hence it is necessary to give an artificial swelling to the milk vein by compressing it at its anterior extremity. The best way is to thrust the end of the finger into the opening through which the milk vein disappears into the body, and we can then determine the size of the vein, for the opening contracts more slowly than the vein.

Most of these indications and signs of good milking qualities in cows are more fully developed after the animals have had several calves, although even with heifers the clever stockman will form some true conclusions. With an eye to beef-making qualities, some desirable features in the udder and milk veins have frequently to be overlooked; yet the purchaser will do wisely to secure as many favourable marks as may be, with other outward signs of a well-made beast. The rumps should lay wide, the hips ditto, and the back display the flatness of a table, while the skin should give the soft feeling to the hand which we will now explain *in extenso*.

The Touch.—It is only the men well educated in

the art of buying cattle that prove judges of touch, and to such men the feeling of the skin and hair of the cow is as important a guide as the rudder to the ship. A clever writer observes—"The touch may be good or bad, fine or harsh, or, as it is often termed, hard or mellow. A thick, firm skin, which is generally covered with a thickset, hard, short hair, always touches hard, and indicates a bad feeder. A thin, meagre, papery skin, covered with thin, silky hair, being the opposite of the one just described, does not, however, afford a good touch. Such a skin is indicative of weakness of constitution, though of good feeding properties. A perfect touch will be found with a thick, loose skin, floating as it were on a layer of soft fat, yielding to the pressure, and springing back towards the fingers, like a piece of soft, thick chamois leather, and covered with thick, glossy, soft hair. Such a collection of hair looks rich and beautiful, and seems warm and comfortable to the animal. It is not unlike a bed of fine soft moss; and hence such a skin is frequently styled 'mossy.' The sensation derived from feeling a fine touch is pleasurable, and even delightful, to an amateur of breeding. You cannot help liking the animal that possesses a fine touch. Along with it is generally associated a fine, symmetrical form. A knowledge of touch can only be acquired by long practice; but, after having acquired it, it is of itself a sufficient means of judging of the feeding quality of the ox; because, when present, the properties of symmetrical form, fine bone, sweet disposition, and purity of blood are the general accompaniments."

Unfortunately it is too frequently found that good milking qualities are not met in conjunction with the signs indicative of good form. The best milkers are often indeed badly shaped, lean, raw-boned, and in no way distinguished as beautiful. Hence, then, the danger there is in choosing from a herd of cows the most beautiful as the best milkers. On the contrary, we not unusually find that in a good milk cow the hind quarters are defective in form, being largely developed; flesh too little in proportion to the bone, so that the bones and haunches protrude. The pelvis is wide, and the hind legs are wide apart to afford space for the udder; the muscles are slender, and the buttocks and thighs small and narrow. The breeder must sacrifice milk rather than introduce such a cow into his herd, or the steers reared from this kind of stock would be ill adapted to fill the stalls, and be made up at three or four years old for the good ripe Christmas beef for which England has justly gained renown. Still by good judgment and perseverance in tracing out the qualities for milk-producing and beef-making, both may be very fairly combined. Such animals on the majority of breeding farms are the best class to keep. There are other breeds which are eminently adapted for certain localities, but year by year the well-bred shorthorns take the position of even our other cherished breeds; and ere the present century has passed away we anticipate that the Durham cattle will well occupy the major part of our pasture-land.

Ireland, too, is becoming fast alive to the advantages of such blood, and if the sons of Erin would cease their riotous conduct, and employ themselves largely in cattle-rearing of the better kind, there is no reason why they should not become quite as prosperous as their English neighbours. The face of the pastures in many parts of

Ireland ever show a verdancy; and such rich and luxuriant herbage as prevails during the spring, summer, and autumn months are eminently suited for breeding, rearing, dairying, and fatting such noble animals as the shorthorn.

Seeing, then, that such herds of beasts as we have described in this chapter are the most profitable kind for the breeder and rearer to keep, they will further improve them at little extra expense by continually using a really good pure-bred Durham sire. Thus in years to come a herd of beasts will be formed very nearly pure bred; a herd that any man may well be proud of, and one sure to prove remunerative to the owner under judicious treatment.

The Dairyman's or Milkseller's Cow.

The animals needed for this purpose are those that will give an abundance of milk. Quality is not so much the object as quantity; and although it is desirable that an animal should be bought that looks like holding its money together, yet size, uniform appearance, and colour must give way to such a one that will fill the bucket. These free milkers are not found amongst the better class of shorthorns, and the Hertfords must be totally discarded for this purpose. The Alderney's milk is rich, but not plentiful enough for the milkseller; so long as no adulteration is practised, milk is milk, will stand the test, and bring in the "coppers." The hardier Welsh excels more in

Ayrshire.

the richness of its milk than its plenteousness, while the small Ayrshire is nearer approaching what is required, being a wonderful milker as far as it goes, but unfortunately, being of such diminutive size, does not go far enough. No cow, however, in the British Isles gives more milk according to its weight than the Ayrshire.

Where, then, are we to look for the beau ideal of a cow that shall give such a plenteous supply of milk as to make the selling of it profitable to the cowkeeper? Probably amongst all the above, or rather from a general mixture of blood. Some of the best milkers we have ever had have been strongly dashed with the Ayrshire blood, the other parts being shorthorns and Alderneys. The first cross between the two latter kinds is hard to beat, providing a good strain on either or on both sides is chosen. Here the Alderney male should be used to mate the shorthorned cow. There is an extraordinary breed of cows for milk of the race *Flamande* or *Flemish*; these, however, are not British animals. The best and purest specimens of these are found in France, and are to be met with on the rich pasture-land in the districts of Hazebrouck, De Bergue of Bailleul, and Cassel. It is the favourite animal of the north to north-east of France, and especially of the celebrated districts of East and West Flanders. It owes its origin probably to the same source as that of the Holland cow. Generally speaking, in their native country, the Flemish cows are kept permanently in the cowhouses, being allowed a run in the stubble fields when the crops have been cleared off in early autumn. Here they are either tethered or attended by the lads or lasses of the district, for hedges or fences are few and far between. In some districts, however, these animals are depastured in the field during the day and sheltered at night; and at Bergue, near Dunkirk, they are pastured out night and day for the summer months. This fine herd of milking cows are now being improved by crossing with our shorthorns and the Normandy breed; the combination having for its aim to impart to the animals the facility to be readily fatted (which distinguishes the English shorthorn), the fineness of the tissues, and the milk-giving faculties of the Flamande, and to retain the milk-giving properties of the Normandy breed, while toning down its coarseness. The Flemish blood might be used to mix with our home breeds, but would sadly reduce the value of the carcase, while it improved the aptitude for milking. This is a consideration, for, although a plentiful supply of milk should be the prior object, yet some sort of regard should be paid to what the animal will make when sold out dry to the farmer or grazier for breeding from again, or for fatting purposes.

The London milkman requires not only free milkers, but such animals as will hold their flesh, and go off direct to the butcher when they no longer answer for milking. Therefore these milksellers buy all the best cows in the autumn time that can be procured. These animals must be fat, or they will not pass for the London market, and large-framed animals with promising udders are much preferred. They are required to give three gallons of milk at a meal, and this they often do for some months, for the food-supply consists of everything that will produce milk, without regard to expense. The object is to force the milk supply and keep the cows fat at the same time, and no sooner does the milk diminish than they are sent off to the butcher, and the stalls are filled with a new importation from the rich pastoral farms of Warwickshire, Northamptonshire, and Leicestershire. Grazing cows for the London milk market has been one of the most remunerative occupations associated with farming for the last two decades. Warwickshire, particularly, is favourably suited for grazing these cows, as, in addition to its rich pastures, warm strawyards are provided for the winter season. This shelter is needed, as the beasts have to be bought in during early winter, served by the bull and be sold out done calving, or with calf at foot, between the 1st September and Christmas. In most other towns, aside from London, a lower class of animals is used, which are milked out and sold, much reduced in flesh, to the farmers, to fatten or breed from again.

The purchaser of these milking cows is not particular to a year or two in the age. Usually animals showing a few wrinkles in the horns give a more plenteous supply of milk than heifers with their first calves; and as the traders in milk only keep the animals, as a rule, during one year, they do not deteriorate much on hand if they have passed their best. Still even here anything approaching a worn-out creature must not be invested in, for however great may be the show of milk, the worn-out constitution, weakened by age, will assuredly prevent the animal from proving remunerative.

We do not counsel milk-sellers to adhere to any fixed breed or cross-breed, but rather prefer several mixtures of blood in animals that show light flesh, and many of the good qualifications for giving milk which we described in the last chapter. It may be looked upon as an established fact that richness of milk will be best procured through the Alderney blood; hardness of constitution through the Welsh; large frame and aptitude to feed from the shorthorn; and quantity of milk through the Ayrshire.

The Constitution.—This is the next matter for consideration, and, though it applies to all animals, three-fourths of the cow-buyers fail to investigate sufficiently closely into it. A large milk return will not be given long unless the cow is in perfect health. The drain on the system is only utilising nature's laws, and may be kept up in a healthy animal if it is supplied with generous diet; but if the constitution becomes weakened by age or any other infirmity, or the feed is dealt out too sparingly, or of an unwholesome character, the milk fonts will decline their office, and shortly cease to produce at all.

A good milk cow should, in addition to the signs indicative of active development of the mammary glands, possess those of good digestive organs, large lungs, and prominent chest. The appetite should be good for solid and wholesome food, not, as is sometimes the case, depraved, so that the animal is desirous of devouring all kind of innutritious matters. The inclination for fluid should be strong, as such a desire is promoted by an abundant flow of milk. When these signs are present the cow makes good blood, so that activity is given to the whole nervous system; the organs are rendered animated, and the gland amply provided with the material necessary for a copious secretion. Possessed of all these characteristics, cows give much milk for a lengthened period, and sometimes possess the additional advantage of fattening rapidly after they become dry.

It happens frequently, however, that activity in the mammary glands is united with the bodily characteristics the opposite of those now named, so that we find cows abundant milkers which have the ribs closely set, the brisket narrow, the digestive organs delicate, the appetite only moderate, but the thirst frequently great; with such signs the milk may be large in quantity but it is poor in quality, and the animals are liable to suffer from lung disease. These kinds of animals are very often shy breeders, although they display the usual natural restlessness at intervals. They are also "ill-thrivers" even when in apparently good health, and when not yielding much milk. Still, good milking cows sometimes turn up in all kinds of three-cornered shapes.

As a good milk-producer, without regard to anything further, Mr. Mayne gives the following description:—
" As regards the general appearance of the cow, preference in all cases should be given to those whose form is furthest removed from that of the male. They should possess, then, (1) a small bony development; (2) fine and slender legs; (3) the head should be small and somewhat long, and get narrow as it approaches the region of the horns; (4) the horns should be of a clear colour and transparent, should taper gradually to the extremities; (5) the skin should be soft, and covered with fine soft and shining clear hair; (6) the natural passages should be provided with a soft silky down; (7) the neck should be small; (8) the shoulders slender, especially near the head; (9) eyelids not much shrivelled; (10) the eyes prominent and bright, but with a mild, feminine expression."

The following will, however, perhaps be more generally received by English cow-keepers as the truer specimen of a dairy cow. "The milk cow should have a long thin head (?), with a brisk but placid eye, be thin and hollow in the neck, narrow in the breast and point of the shoulder, and altogether light in the forequarter, but wide in the loins, with little dewlap, and neither too full fleshed along the chine, nor showing in any part an indication to put on much fat. The udder should be especially large, round, and full, with the milk veins protruding, yet thin-skinned, but not hanging loose or tending far behind. The teats should also stand square, all pointing out at equal distances, and of the same size; and although neither very large nor thick towards the udder, yet long and tapering to a point. A cow with a large head, a high backbone, a small udder and teats, and drawn up in the belly, will, beyond all doubt, be found a bad milker." It is important that the temperament of a milk cow should be considered, for it is a bad sign when the animal is habitually restive or uneasy when the milking process is going on. On the contrary, she should have all the appearance of being happy during the operation, and the greatest kindness on the part of the attendant is essential; it is singular how instinctively a cow discriminates between one who is careful to her or otherwise. It loves to be fondled, and in return caresses its master.

The kind milking cow will be observed to chew its cud while the milking process is going on almost invariably when not feeding. Some cows that are in the habit of suspending their milk will give it down quite freely when fed with some tempting morsel when the process is going on. Care in all these things is essential; and if regard is not paid to them, good cows will be spoiled.

The master should ever be present during milking-time, and nothing that goes on amiss should escape his vigilant eye. Conducted under such management, milk-selling is a good business, providing the market or station is near; but otherwise expenses eat up all profit. It is not in our opinion generally known how nutritious a fluid milk is, or it would be more largely used. It is wholesome for all persons either in health or illness, and the more children live on it the better. Even skim milk has valuable nutritious qualities, and should in some way or other be more freely conveyed to the centres of vast cities. Millions of gallons of skim milk are annually given to pigs, which often do not answer to pork; while if it were conveyed to large towns, it would be a perfect boon to mothers who have families to provide for. While no food could be more wholesome, neither could any other be obtained at so cheap a rate. Expense of conveyance is the one great burden now, and railway companies would do well to reduce their charges for such commodities, and then the occupation of cow-keeping for milk-selling would be rapidly sought after, more milk would be submitted to the public, and the community at large be benefited by it.

The Cottier's Cow.

The cows are here needed that will subsist upon hard fare at times, and exist upon the paddock or orchard, with little other change perhaps than an occasional run along the roadside to graze the sparse herbage which is there to be found. In some instances they get a wider range, it is true, on lean grass fields, or on the over-stocked common, where only cows of a hard kind could find support. Still, thousands of animals are kept under such circumstances in England, Wales, Scotland, and Ireland, and very much help the well-to-do peasant to live in a more comfortable manner, while the poorer neighbours are benefited from the spare milk-supply. In many cases the owner is the thrifty servant who has saved sufficient from his hard-earned gains to purchase a cow, and from one the number may be increased under favourable circumstances to two or three. It is, however, to be regretted that at other times impartial disease seizes the much-cherished animal, and does not relinquish its grasp until death has claimed the victim for its own. Such cases are sad indeed, and all the hard-gotten gains of the peasant are wrested from him at one fell swoop. We have found, from careful experience, that cows kept upon limited spaces of ground are much more liable to diseases than when they are allowed to roam over wider pastures. These animals need change of food, and one plant counteracts any evil results that may arise from another, providing the range of ground is sufficiently wide to supply the antidote. The ranunculus or buttercup has been greatly condemned by some stock-owners, and veterinary surgeons too, as being the cause of red water and other malignant diseases. It may tend to such complaints if eaten by an animal of depraved appetite, but a creature in health only takes just sufficient to help to digest other food.

How a practical man can retain the doctrine that this plant is poisonous we are at a loss to explain —considering all the richest pastures in England abound with the herb. Such lands as a rule are reputed as being particularly wholesome and nutritious for horned cattle. Again, if this species of herbage is so poisonous, wherefore is it that no injury arises from animals taking hay containing great quantities of the supposed deadly plants? If mankind would reason and commune with nature a little more, and leave her laws to take their course, a much more correct conclusion would be arrived at. The fact is, that when the young free-growing grasses of spring first prevail, they contain much watery sap, and if taken largely by the bovine species which have been wintered on dry food, the sudden change is likely to cause colic, or hoven, or blown, and inflammation might follow. Howbeit in many pastures the buttercup or ranunculus at this season carpets the whole face of the earth like a cloth of gold. Animals will scarcely take the plant in by choice, but it is impossible for them to feed without occasional flowers or branches mingling with the grasses. The buttercup is of a hot and most acrid nature, and mixing with the cold grasses, stimulates the stomach into action, and thus assists digestion—indeed it acts upon a cow much as a glass of spirits would do upon a human being. Towards midsummer, when the grasses become more wholesome, the buttercups depart, leaving only a few hard stems which cattle refuse to take—neither does their stomach then need any stimulant to aid the digestion of the fast-maturing grasses.

To return to the subject in hand: As the cottier's cow is more liable to disorder than such as roam at large, and considering that he can less afford to lose his animal, as probably with it would go his all, it would be well if the more opulent classes would assist him to insure against such disasters.

The poor man's choice of a cow is between three breeds; viz., the Ayrshire, the Welsh, and the Kerry. The Alderney has been tried many times, but found wanting in constitution, being unable to rough it, as the peasant's animal ever has to do. The Ayrshire will doubtless thrive on a less span of land than any other breed; in a previous part of this work we have commented upon its many advantages.

The Welsh cows are most hardy, and may be roughly defined between the North and South "Walers." The northern animals are of a hardier, coarser breed, having much more hair to protect them against the cutting winds than their southern neighbours, which are much more highly prized for dairy purposes.

Those termed Pembrokes, from being bred in Pembrokeshire, are the pick of the country for milk produce, butter-making, and for fattening for the butcher when milked out. The flesh is well mixed, and held in repute for its good quality; but Welsh cattle do not generally appear to be improved, or rather, there is actually a deterioration of late years, arising in no small degree from the circumstance that the breeders in Wales have for some time been selling their best heifers for fattening purposes, instead of retaining them to breed from. Such a system is enough to destroy any breed. By careful selection of the heifers, and a due attention to the character of the bulls which are used, much improvement might be effected in the cattle breed in the mountainous districts of Wales; and with this there might be an infusion of other blood derived from a mountain breed, the best for the purpose being the Argyleshire and West Highland. The true colour of Welsh cattle is black, without any white, and the horns are fine, turned upwards at the points, and tipped with black.

The Welsh cattle have hard constitutions, and will live on land where others would starve; some of them have also the advantage of retaining their supply of milk longer than almost any other beasts. It is not uncommon to milk them quite round, *i.e.*, until they calve again. Howbeit this is ever a reprehensible practice, and will, if repeated, spoil any cow. These animals only need housing during the coldest nights in winter, and even in the dead of that season are better pastured by day.

Of the Kerry we can but speak favourably; and it is no doubt well suited for the cowkeeper who has a limited space to pasture upon. While these animals are not so hardy as the Welsh, and therefore not so fitted for exposure and northern localities, still they will endure more hardships than our English breeds.

"The Kerry cow is as small as a cow of the Scottish skibos, and somewhat similar to her in points and shape. She is, comparative to her size, a very copious milker; and she possesses the same kind of reputation throughout a large portion of Ireland which belongs to the Ayrshire cow in the western districts of the Scottish lowlands. Kerry heifers are in constant demand at comparatively high prices, and they may be met in droves, in many parts of the low country, ready to be sold in pairs or one by one to the small farmers of the rural districts, the cow-keepers and milk-sellers in towns. Kerry cattle, when unmolested or very gently treated, are perfectly quiet; but when disturbed or even slightly irritated, they break all bounds and overleap every ordinary fence." A second writer observes: "The Kerry is an Irish breed of great value, both for dairy purposes and the value of the beef when fattened. It has, however, been sadly neglected. Kerry cattle are small, many of the cows not exceeding, and being sometimes under, forty inches in height at the shoulder. Their milk is rich, and when fattened the beef is fine-grained and well mixed. Black is the general colour, but black and white and brown or brindled are also common colours. The cows are gentle (?), and while suited for poor mountain pastures, they are also an appropriate description for the villa farm."

Leaving, then, the small cowkeeper to make his choice between the above breeds, which he will from locality and other prevailing circumstances be best able to do, we will now close this part of our work for other matters also demanding attention.

Definition of Age.

It is of the first importance that the purchasers of cows should be conversant with the signs of their ages. The rough and ready scowl-of-brow conclusions that certain men use is not sufficient in many instances, and other more truthful indications must be sought for. It is requisite to be able to mark the signs of youth as well as age, for the young animals may be spoiled by being bred from too soon, or by being exposed to ill-judged hardship, while the old should be disposed of at a certain period before they have far advanced on the downward path of life.

The mammary glands of cows, like all other organs,

DEFINITION OF AGE.

develop themselves in proportion to the exercise of their functions: hence it happens that a cow does not give so much milk after its first or second calf as after the third or fourth, although the milk is never richer than after the first birth has taken place. The question of quantity holds more especially true in cases where the heifer has been bred from at too early an age. It may be taken as a fact, then, that the cow yields its maximum of milk after several calvings, and after being long treated to a good system of management. It is scarcely a good plan to buy five or six year old cows at fairs or markets, for it rarely happens that they are sold at reasonable prices at this age, if free from faults; and, further, they will shortly begin to go downhill.

It is obvious, then, that in judging the value of a milk cow, it is particularly of importance to be able to determine its age, for after it has reached a certain period of life its milking capabilities are decreased. A cow when she has had her fourth calf, or in her sixth year, may be said to have reached her best point; after which the milking qualities will get yearly less valuable. The flow of milk may be pretty well kept up, but the quality will become much deteriorated, and the animal more quickly goes dry after calving when advanced in years.

The horns and the teeth afford ready and sufficiently accurate means to determine the age of a cow. The horns vary much in size and in general appearance; but in all their annual growth is indicated by a ring — when the calf is one year old — more or less visible. The sign of the first year of the calf's existence is a "circular depression between the skin and the bulging horn;" that of the second year, a "second bulge, with a depression below it;" that of the third year, a "third bulge, with a depression below it." These marks, or annular bulges and depressions, are, however, by no means easily observed; and it is not till the third year that the mark is distinct. Culley, in his celebrated treatise on "Live Stock," says that the first wrinkle upon the horn does not take place until three years old, after which they get another circle or wrinkle every year as long as the horn stands on, though not always equally discernible in all horned cattle; and stock-owners generally believe in Culley's doctrine. We are sorry to say that it is too common for jobbers and cow-dealers to scrape, rasp, or file down these wrinkles in old cattle to prevent the age being known, and by that means to deceive and impose upon the unwary, the ignorant, and the unsuspicious; and this process is called among the fraternity "bishoping." In reckoning the age of a cow, then, by the circles on the horn, they should be counted from that nearest to the tip and point, and as the last well-developed circle will be the third (this, as stated above, being the first which is plainly observable), two more will have to be added to the number. Thus, if there are five well-developed circles, the last furthest from the tip of the horn will be the third year's circle; so that, reckoning the two first years, the age of the animal will be shown to be seven. If there are four well-developed circles the age will be six, if six circles the age will be eight —two being added in all cases to the number of well-developed circles will give the age of the cow.

But, from what we have stated above, it will be noticed that the indications afforded by the circles of the horns cannot always be relied upon, as they are frequently subjected to the tampering of dishonest dealers; and although the same may be said regarding their practices with the teeth in isolated cases, still these are generally taken and relied upon as affording correct enough indications of age. It seems a somewhat strange thing to say, but it is nevertheless true enough, that the indications afforded by the teeth of the age of cows and oxen are less to be depended upon since the improvements made in breeding and feeding than when the animals are in a more natural condition, and this arises from the circumstance that these improvements naturally induce a "precocity of development" and exercise "a modifying influence upon the teeth in common with other parts, and even more particularly upon them as parts of the digestive system." Another cause is much hard food, such as cake, which is now extensively given, and tends to break and wear out the teeth.

Professor Simonds, in his paper on "The Teeth of the Ox, Sheep, and Pig, as indicative of the Age of the Animal," in vol. xv. of the Journal of the Agricultural Society, has thoroughly exhausted the subject, and shown the errors which have crept into our agricultural treatises through insufficient knowledge of the subject. Thus a very general opinion amongst breeders, and which has found a place in several treatises, is, that the ox cannot be said to be "full-mouthed"—that is, possessed of all its teeth—"until it is six years old." Professor Simonds, as the result of a most extended and carefully-made series of observations and investigations, finds, on the contrary, that, "as a rule, even under unfavourable circumstances, the dentition of the ox is completed before the fourth year of his age." The following table of the dentition of the ox is given by this excellent authority :—

Table of Early Average. The breed and other causes favouring development.			Table of Late Average. The breed and other retarding causes of development.		
Years.	Months.		Years.	Months.	
1	9	Two permanent incisors.	2	3	Two permanent incisors.
2	3	Four do.	2	9	Four do.
2	9	Six do.	3	3	Six do.
3	3	Eight do.	3	9	Eight do.

The following remarks and table are taken from Professor Brown's paper on the same subject in the Bath and West of England Agricultural Society's Journal some time ago :—" In all animals whose ages are matters of inquiry, we gain most evidence from the incisors, or front teeth, from the ease with which the appearances may be ascertained; but in any doubtful cases the molars, or back teeth, will be referred to with advantage for the purpose of correcting the opinion. The farmer can, however, hardly be expected to know sufficient of the anatomy of these parts to consult them successfully, although to the professional examiner they are more definite than the incisors, besides being less subject to exceptions, and undergoing very marked changes at a time when the incisors are almost useless as tests. It is satisfactory to be able to add that no authenticated case has occurred in which both incisors and molars have shown exceptional appearances; on the contrary, a peculiarity in the one has been invariably corrected by the absence of it in the other. To enable the stock exhibitor to examine his animals and form an opinion of the condition of their mouths at intervals, the following tabular view of dentition will, it is hoped, suffice. As no average can be taken in many cases, it will be advisable in such to take two or three periods, such as early, late, and ordinary times, for the changes that will be mentioned. Even a fourth period might be permitted to include instances of extreme precocity; but these are so few that no practical benefit could follow their classification, although they may often affect the opinion of the examiner who is familiar with them. To economise space as far as may be, we shall use the letter T for temporary or milk teeth, and P for permanent or adult teeth. The ages in any cases are only pursued as far as the restrictions extend.

Dentition of the Ox.

3 incisors (T) in lower jaw only. 6 molars (T) in both jaws.
8   „   (P)   „   „   12   „   (P)   „   „

Incisors.	Molars.	Early.	Late.	Average.
Eight (T) just pricking up.	Six (T) just pricking in both jaws.	...	...	Birth.
Eight (T) fairly up.	Six (T) fairly up.	...	...	6 weeks.
	4th (P) behind the 3d (T).	...	...	6 months.
Incisors worn and getting apart from each other.	5th (P) behind the above.	...	...	15 months.
Central (P) up, 1st pair (2-toothed).	6th molar behind the above.	1 yr. 6 ms.	2 yrs. 4 ms.	2 years.
Middles, 2d pair (4-toothed).	...	2 yrs. 4 ms.	2 yrs. 8 ms.	2 yrs. 6 ms.
Laterals, 3d pair (6-toothed).	...	2 yrs. 5 ms.	...	3 years.
Corners, 4th pair (8-toothed).	...	2 yrs. 10 ms.	3 yrs. 9 ms.	3 yrs. 6 ms.

"Between the second and third years the three anterior molars are changed for permanent, and their examination is indispensable for the formation of an opinion; during this time the incisors, as will be seen by the table, being subject to extraordinary variations. The remark early and late refers only to the incisors." Those cattle-buyers who do not wish their purchased cows to have more calves, nor to retain them long in their possession, sometimes find it advantageous to buy rather older animals, taking care that they are in good condition and have good teeth. In such instances the condition should not be lost. There is a chance of these animals answering certain purposes; they give a large yield of milk, and when dried off and are well fatted they fetch a pretty good price from the butcher—not, however, so much per lb. as younger animals. There are such other indications of age as loss of teeth, or teeth worn short and standing a distance apart, an overgrown carcase, long bag, and general ancient appearance that at once reminds the experienced cattle-buyer that old age is coming on, and that the milkmaid has sung too many songs under the cow to render such a purchase likely to prove remunerative.

Purchasing.

In laying the foundation of a herd of cows the breeder needs to use his whole stock of knowledge, for as he commences so may he expect to follow on. It is not so easy to correct defects in animals by way of mating them with approved sires as people are apt to imagine; far more easy to engender more faults. It is a common error made in breeding to try and improve a fault that the dam may have, by using a sire that is particularly good about such a point where the dam shows weakness, and at the same time other defects in the sire are overlooked. This proceeding is clearly wrong, for it should be the object to *lose nothing*, while any improvement that can be made should be taken advantage of. As an instance, if a cow has a little slackness of the loin, it would be well to choose a sire extra good in this part, but it would be just an open question if the offspring would prove as correctly made in the same part, while any disapproved make in the sire might, and likely enough would be, imparted to the calf. A sire should be pretty perfectly made, and it is better at all times to sacrifice size than make.

In choosing heifers for a permanent herd, therefore, the buyer should not be too extravagant in his idea of size, or defects in make are almost sure to be overlooked, and they will descend to the offspring pretty well as sure as they are present in the parent. They may not be imparted to the first calf, perhaps not to the first generation, but glaring faults are sure to display themselves sooner or later in the offspring, although they may lie dormant for such a prolonged period that the stock-master has congratulated himself that he is well rid of them. Thus it is that true make must be the first motto, and then as much size as may be. Another rock on which the purchaser is often cast is in buying animals that are too fat, for flesh covers a multitude of defects, and high condition not unfrequently deceives good judges. Rather poor healthy animals that have been subsisting on hard fare improve from the day they are bought, and receiving more generous treatment, please the owner more each visit he makes to them.

THE COW AND THE CALF.

The sleek, high-conditioned animal has, ten to one, been living on all imaginary good food, and languishes under only ordinary treatment. In buying poor, improving cows, *touch*, of which we spoke at length in a previous chapter, must be the grazier's beacon and guide. It is quite easy for the inexperienced to pick up a poor animal which is a confirmed "screw," but in such a case the good qualities of the skin and hair will be ever absent. No sooner does the young beginner enter the market than he is besieged by all the dealers that have "screwy" animals to dispose of, and he is lucky if he escapes them all. These "chafferers" do not try it on with experienced hands, knowing full well that their nefarious tricks will not work there, so their victims are the amateurs. The "screw" will be found to have a dry hard coat, the skin fixed on to the flesh as if glued there; and such signs as dry nostrils, sunken eyes, tucked-up belly, wasted twist, bareness of flesh, and a painful gait in walking. It is often the case that the lungs are the seat of the disorder, and a dry husk or cough will betray the secret. This cough will be brought on by stirring the animal suddenly along. Practical men look upon this sudden movement as a test, and whether it is practised in the fair or field will generally bring on a fit of coughing. Diarrhœa or looseness must be looked upon with suspicion when present in a poor animal, while rumination is a favourable symptom, and seldom practised by a cow far gone in decline. The tail, too, often shows a weak, thin appearance, the bottom part being void of muscular power, hence the ignorant attribute the whole decay of the animal's health to what they are pleased to term tail-worm. So the tail is cut with a pen-knife at the extreme end, the small muscular cords removed—which the operator terms the worm—and the cow is expected at once to return to a state of convalescence. We need scarcely say all this is utter nonsense, for no such thing as tail-worm exists that is supposed to interfere so materially with the health of the cow, and the stupid stockowner might as well expect to cure his animal by cutting a nick in the nearest gate-post. It is really painful to contemplate at the present day the ignorance that exists amongst stockmen and their masters, and nothing prevails more commonly amongst their cattle than imaginary diseases and imaginary cures.

There are a few more common defects to be guarded against in buying beasts, such as partial or total blindness, hips displaced, ill-shaped bags, defective teats, &c. The last peculiarity, however, will not be detected in the maiden heifer. In purchasing a cow that has already calved, the first step will be to take a general view of the animal, and if she appears suitable, to go in for more minute particulars. The age first should be ascertained, for on no account should any one under any pretence be induced to buy an old animal, no matter how tempting the price may be, for they decline on hand, and always turn out too dear. Few people would credit the extra food that old animals take. The "touch" of the cow should next be proved satisfactory, and then the udder carefully examined. Each teat must not only give milk, but the same free stream should flow from all. If the milk runs of itself from the teats, suspicions may be had that the cow sheds her milk. This is objectionable; in such instances dealers take care to keep the udder pretty empty. Small tumours often form in the passage of the teats, which

D

may or may not later on cause the loss of the quarters where they are located. These tumours can be detected, even when very small, by carefully passing the finger and thumb over the milk passage. By standing in front of the animal, a good idea will be formed of the fore part, consisting of the head, neck, and brisket, or chest. It is, however, behind where the judge loves to take a general survey, for from such a situation the rumps, hips, loin, ribs, and chine will at once come under view. If there is one thing more essential than another—in not only a cow, but in all other animals—it is a good set of ribs. They should not be flat, but evenly placed well back into the loin, in barrel shape, or well curved. In the cow the back rib is of vast importance. It is considered a great point with the butcher, and is about the first part that his hand is put upon. Other particulars of the proper shape, &c., of the cow will be found elsewhere in this volume. The question of colour is of importance to the breeder who intends rearing his stock, while to those who do not intend rearing calves, but selling off fat, colour is not of paramount importance. The breeder, however, chooses such colours as deep reds, reds and whites, light roans, strawberry roans, and avoids dark nostrils. Thus the offspring will prove of good colour also. A neat head, gay colour, with jaunty gait, adds much to the appearance of the beast, and such qualities so attract the eyes of customers that a higher price is paid, the purchaser knowing full well that they never adorn the mongrel-bred cow.

It is preferable to buy stock on the farm where they are bred, if possible, as not only are animals often injured through the abuse of drovers at fairs and markets, but a risk of taking or creating disease is run, and in pregnant animals abortion is often brought about. The manner in which cattle are abused in our fairs and markets is a crying disgrace to the enlightened age in which we live, and it is high time the police authorities bestirred themselves in the matter, for they are empowered to do so; indeed, it is their duty. Blows are applied as if the poor creatures have no feeling, and over-driving without food or water is commonly practised.

If purchasing could be done on the home farms, besides the above evils being avoided, all middle men would be shut out, for whom there is no spare profit in these depressed days of farming; animals would be more healthy, and many contagious and other diseases would be avoided. The last general closing of fairs owing to the prevalence of "foot-and-mouth disease" proved this, for not only was this disease arrested in its progress, but other contagious ones also disappeared from our herds and flocks. Every experienced grazier knows how often cows are bought that have been driven from fair to fair until they are so footsore and jaded that they are half a summer before they commence to thrive and lay on flesh. Therefore the grass season passes away, while they are not nearly made up for the butcher; the only resource being left is expensive stall-feeding, or selling out at little, if any, over cost price. Buying and selling stock at home is then to be commended in every way. The advantages to the seller are that they never look so well in any other position, and therefore he gets the best price without paying any outpocket expenses whatever, while the advantages to the buyer chiefly are that the animals are healthy, resty, and in a good state to go on immediately they are removed to fresh quarters.

Treatment during Gestation.

Approved animals having been bought in, we will now consider their further treatment. Assuming that a herd of maiden heifers have been purchased in the spring time, at the age of two years, just as the grass fields begin to display a verdant face. After the animals have laid a month and become settled to their pastures, it will be time to mate them with an approved sire. We are now advising for the breeder's herd. A young sire is essential here, say from twelve to eighteen months old; and to ensure the fruitfulness of all the animals, he should lie with the herd, or within measurable distance. Otherwise the shepherd, upon whom attention to these matters generally falls, fails to interest himself to take the heifers to a distance, and thus a portion of the herd prove unfruitful from neglect. When in a healthy state, cows usually come in use every fortnight or three weeks until impregnated, and their period of gestation is forty-one weeks—a few days more or less. The heifers would calf down from two years and nine months old to three years. For the breeder, under all circumstances, this is quite early enough, although for the dairyman or milk-seller six months younger would be considered a good age to have the first calf. No doubt breeding from animals too young stops their growth. Sometimes bad times calving result, while the first calf is often but an undersized creature, totally unfit to bring into the herd. It should, however, be understood that heifers that have been well cared for the whole of their lives are as forward at eighteen months old as others that have subsisted on less generous diet, or that have been neglected, are at two years, so that the graziers may best judge when to commence breeding from the animals under their care.

The sire should be of pure shorthorned blood, and an animal as near perfect shape as possible. Extra size may be passed over, a mass of fat is not needed; but stainless blood, good make, and colour are *sine qua non* to the improvement of the herd. If a pretty numerous one, the owner will best serve his own interest by keeping a bull on the farm; but in cases where only several cows are kept, why this will scarcely answer, and the services of the neighbour's must be utilised.

During gestation the quiet field is the best place until winter sets in, but it is above all things requisite that the animals should not be subject to fright. The wild yelping cur of a sheep-dog, or any other of the canine species, should not be allowed to disturb the quiet of the herd, for nothing would be more likely to bring on cases of untimely birth. The water supply should be pure and wholesome; and it is the exception rather than the rule to find such the case in the common pasture-fields. Too often stagnant pools, offensive to the smell, are the only drinking-places that cattle have to quench their thirst at. The bottom of the pond probably contains the relics of fallen and decayed branches and leaves of many years' accumulation from trees above or around the pond. The excretion and urine of many a herd of beasts have been added to the filthy fluid, for many a summer the gadfly (*Œstrus bovis*) or the heat has driven the excited and panting herd into the water, while many a pond is made a general sepulchre for all animals that die in its immediate vicinity. Is it a wonder, then, that diseases prevail in our land? No; but it is marvellous that more dire maladies do not rage than is now the case. The nearest way to produce an unhealthy system is foul water, and the most fruitful method of causing abortion amongst any pregnant animals is ill-health.

The food while animals are upon a summer pasture consists wholly of grass; and if the plants are healthy, nothing is more wholesome for the breeding cow. Howbeit there is a disease now common to our grasses known as ergot, which in wet seasons produces more cases of abortion than any other one cause; and this fact is far too little known and understood by the ordinary stock-keeper. Ergot is a parasitic fungus that fixes itself on the grasses in the shape of a minute balloon-like germ. This germ lodges on the bloom of the grasses, taking possession of the small cavity provided for the grass-seed. Here the germ grows into a dark-brown or black spur, varying from a quarter of an inch to three quarters of an inch in length, and in thickness varying between that of a fine needle and a wheat-grain. It is characteristic of the plant that it invariably grows in the shape of a cock's spur, hence the French gave it the name of ergot. Eaten in sufficient quantities, it causes inflammation of the uterus or womb of any pregnant animal, when abortion usually results. Breeding cows should be removed from pastures which are so diseased. Spurs are not often detected before the latter end of July or the beginning of August, so that before this time the poisonous parasite need not be feared, and it is never found to any extent upon meadows after they have been mown. Therefore the farmer can always remove his cows from the ergoted uplands to insure a healthy pasture on the mown pastures. The hay should be examined in winter time, as the spurs sometimes prevail amongst it.

In the winter season the pregnant cow needs more attention. First, the food must all be of a light, wholesome, but nutritious character. It is essential that animals should come down calving in good condition, or there will be small hopes of a profitable dairy cow. The hay must be neither overgrown or weather-beaten in the field, and neither mouldy or overheated in the rick. The best hay is such as holds the fragrance of that newly made in summer time;—so much the better if the colour is not changed. Roots are quite wholesome diet given in moderation, and in a matured state; indeed, they are requisite where the animals cannot get a run to pasture for a few hours during the day. Mangel-wurzel are unfit to use before Christmas—better to be withheld until past Lady-day. Some veterinary surgeons deem them poisonous before Christmas. Carrots are a most wholesome root at all times, and should be more widely cultivated by the farmer. Ground oats or three or four pounds of mixed linseed and cotton-cake are wholesome food, and beans, peas, and rice meal may be given in judicious quantities. It is better to underfeed rather than overfeed, and the man who breeds from animals that he intends keeping on need not force them into such high condition as if they had to be sold to dealers. Indeed, really prime hay and roots are sufficient in themselves, but if straw is mixed with the hay in the chopping process a little meal or cake may be required. The roots should always be pulped and mixed with some chaff until they begin to ferment; thus the food is served up in a slightly warm state, when it is much more wholesome for the cow's stomach than when taken in cold.

Second, the water must be pure; but we do not approve of it taken from the cold spring. If it is too hard and cold, it should stand in some warmer temperature for twelve hours before it is given. Cold spring water served out to a thirsty cow living upon dry food is positively unwholesome, and still more so if the animal has just been feeding on cold roots. It is better to take the water from a clear stagnant pool; but the best water of all is clear soft water, or rain-water when taken pure; and cows love it better than any other. Many a washing-woman has plied the broom freely to the poor dairy cow that has made too free at the soft-water butt. Nature's laws are always displayed by animals, if their owners would but study their habits. It would be better if buildings were so arranged that all rain-water could be saved for cattle; the extra outlay would thus be repaid over and over again in a few years.

Third, exercise is requisite for the cow during gestation, and a few hours' run in the pasture-field during the day all winter is desirable. In such cases they get a little grass and seek their own drinking-places. The shed or yards should be cool and well ventilated, or the animals will feel too severely the chill in the pastures. Cool yards promote the growth of a warm garment in the shape of hair, and when this is put on cows seldom take cold. It is folly to tie animals by the neck during gestation, even during the night. A comfortable roomy bed on a high and dry spot should always be provided, and if under an open shed so much the better. It is most important that heifers should not lie too crowded, for they are far more spiteful than older cows or steers; and any more than usually quarrelsome one should be removed to other quarters. It is a good practice to tie them up while they are taking their extra food, such as cake, roots, and any other diet that they are likely to fight over.

Fourth, no frights or disturbance should be allowed, and no bad smells should prevail. The attendant should be a steady, trustworthy, good-tempered man, one who feeds his animals punctually, and is fond of and takes delight in his work. These men are now difficult to procure, and any one getting hold of such should pay them well, for many a herdsman wastes more than his week's wages come to during the week who has a quantity of stock to attend to. When cows have passed half their time of gestation their food should be of a more generous kind, or they will be found to decline in flesh, having the living fœtus then to support.

Treatment during Parturition.

In cases of heifers bringing their first calves, little if any change of treatment is required until they calve. In winter they should lie in a roomy yard, be frequently watched, and in summer the precaution should be taken that those whose time is accomplished do not lie in a field where treacherous watering-places exist, such as brooks, rivers, and ponds. If these watery graves could render up an account of their dead, they would amount to myriads. Often the thirsty mother goes to drink before the calf can scarcely stagger along, and upon blundering over the river bank has little power to save itself. Ponds may be easily so mounded that no fear need arise from such a loss, but how seldom are these important matters considered on the farm! Young lambs and foals also at times share the same ill fate of drowning.

When the heifer shows signs of calving, " the *labia pudendi*—or external shape—increases in size, and discharges a thick viscid mucus; the mammary gland becomes swelled, hot, and full of colostrum, or the first milk; and, what is always regarded by the breeder as an immediate forerunner of delivery, the ligaments of the pelvis give way, or, to use the farmer's language, the cow is *down in her bones.*" Delivery being at hand, the animal displays great pain and restlessness, lies down quickly, only, however, to as quickly rise; labour pains come on at first in a slight degree, but later on grow in intensity even until delivery is complete. Although it is desirable to render some assistance, more particularly to heifers, yet too much haste must not be used, for the heifer needs much more time than the cow that has had several calves. The *amnion*, or, as it is commonly called, the water-bladder, is first presented, and this should be ruptured by the attendant, when, if natural delivery is taking place, the forefeet and nose of the calf shortly are presented. The forelegs being just protruded, the head will be observed resting upon them about the knees. Assistance should now be rendered, and the birth will be at once accomplished. Should any unnatural position of the calf be observed, the veterinary surgeon should be called in. In too many instances both master and servant are in too great haste and fear evil consequences, when if only a little more patience was exercised all would be well; and this more often occurs with heifers, which frequently require three or four hours.

When the mother has been safely delivered, if in the genial days of summer, she may be brought into a cool shed at night and have given to her a bran-mash a little chilled, or rain-water, and the bag must be eased if painfully full. It must now be ascertained if the calf has sucked: if so, it will look after itself for the future; but if it has not, it must be assisted to the udder. There is, however, seldom much difficulty with the young calf, for it is by no means a delicate or tender creature—very different in such respects to a foal. We do not approve of milking the bag quite out for the first two or three days after calving; such is contrary to nature's course, and might lead to parturient apoplexy —still more is the practice to be condemned of milking before the birth has taken place. The first milk taken after calving, called colostrum, is too rich for forming a cream and making butter, therefore is kept apart from the other milk for the first three days; this richness is seen more in the heifers' than in older cows'. The umbilical cord or navel string of the calf is generally— we may say almost always—ruptured or broken in the act of giving birth; and should such not be the case, it will be sure to break when the cow gets on her legs or the calf is moved. This natural breaking of the navel string is far preferable to the herdman or attendant severing it. The placenta or after-birth is withheld a few hours, and should be removed from the presence of the cow immediately it falls away, but must not be forced away from the animal. In severe weather in winter a large airy loose-box, with plenty of clean litter, is the best place for both cow and calf for the first week, when the calf is generally weaned. Chilled water, bran-mashes, pulped roots, with a little sweet hay, form proper food for the newly-calved cow in the winter season, when green herbage is not procurable. The more aged cow requires a little different treatment, particularly when parturient apoplexy is suspected. Then the food-supply for a week or a fortnight before calving should be of a sparse kind, and several doses of mild purging medicine may be given. When one dose has worked off another may be administered. After calving the same precaution should be taken for the first week, when danger from this malady will be past. Heifers seldom if ever suffer from this fearful malady, and upon certain land older cows are seldom known to be attacked. Therefore we do not advise purging and such artificial means to be used, unless an attack is suspected. Free milkers full of flesh, and more particularly the Alderney breed, after the second calf, are the most liable to "fall." We counsel that the calf should remain with the cow as well as the heifer for a week after birth. Thus the youngster has the advantage of sucking at frequent intervals and getting the colostrum, so needful to its tender stomach. An exception to this rule may be made with the milk-seller's cow, where the milk is more valuable than the calf; but where the calf is of value the mother's milk should not be withheld. The calf should also lie loose with its mother, when it will suck at frequent intervals—a much more commendable plan than being fasted twelve hours and then perhaps being supplied with inferior milk. In the summer season it is not desirable to separate the heifer or cow as a rule from the herd until signs of delivery are observable; and even then it is better for the birth to take place in the open field, for suddenly removing the animal does not tend to hasten labour. When cows calve that are intended for sale, they are just as well left in the paddock night and day, the only thing being needed is that their bags should be eased when showing signs of being too much extended with milk. In instances where the calf is fattened, after the first week the youngster gets milk twice a day, is kept up in a small pen, and either takes its milk direct from the cow, or the milk may be milked into a vessel and then be given. The latter plan is the better one so far as the cow's condition is concerned.

Food for Dairy Cows.

Whether our readers are the owners of single cows, to which they look for a supply of good wholesome milk for their families—whether they are dairymen supplying towns, or dairy farmers in remoter country districts, we would desire to impress each of them with the importance of treating their cows liberally with regard to food; reminding them, that whatever tends to render the yield of cows less than it should be, recoils on the owners, no matter whatever particular breed of cattle they may prefer, and that in all cases "the cream comes by the mouth."

In the feeding of dairy cows, four main points must be kept in view—1st, to aid the increase of milk; 2d, to improve the quality of the milk; 3d, to maintain the condition of the cow; 4th, to produce manure of high quality. Too often the careless dairyman only looks as far as his milk-pail is concerned, and fails to notice that his cow is wasting flesh day by day, until at last the milk falls off, and the beast has to be dried much sooner than she need have been under more judicious treatment. Sweet, well-harvested hay that is got in the latter end of June or first week in July is the very best quality, providing it is not gathered in too quickly to heat in the stack. Grass cut at the above season contains the maximum of sap. Most of the plants are in full bloom, and therefore the crop is in its proper state for cutting. Grass is not the most nutritious when the seed is ripe. Many of the seeds are dislodged in haymaking, and the remainder of the plant is woody, indigestible, and innutritious, thus such fodder is particularly unwholesome for the dairy cow. Clover-hay, when well got, is supposed to be a better milk-provider than meadow-hay; but, in the writer's opinion, this would much depend upon the sort of land the hay was cut from. Howbeit, it is sufficient for us to observe, that either meadow or clover hay is wholesome for the dairy cow when well harvested, and must, when the grass season is over, form the principal food. Bran stands very high in the list of good milk-producers. It increases the flow of milk, improves its quality, and holds up the condition of the cow, while no unpleasant flavour is imparted to the butter; it is also a cheap diet. This food should be given warm in mash shape, and two gallons per day will be a good allowance with other food. Oats are very similar in favourable results to wheaten bran, and may be given from one to one and a half gallons, with other food, per day. In most instances it is needful to have them crushed, or they pass whole, when of course no nutriment is obtained from them, beside the pain and inconvenience felt by the cows in passing undigested food. Bean and pea meals tend more to improve the carcase of the animal than to increase the milk-supply; while, if given too freely, an unpleasant flavour is given to the butter. Therefore we only advise these meals to be used very sparingly amongst other mixtures. Linseed-cake is rich in both milk and flesh-producing qualities, and gives no bad taste to the butter, unless used in too large quantities. Cotton-cake is still more strongly advised; it is cheaper than linseed, produces nearly as much milk, and does not make the butter strong. Both these cakes render milk of high quality. Rice-meal, when got pure, is strongly advised for cows. It needs, however, to be purchased at wholesale price from large firms, for such as is obtained in odd sacks is often much adulterated. This meal tends to sweeten all other food, in addition to its own nutritious qualities, and is best mixed with pulped roots and chaff. Roots need using with caution. Swedes, when well matured, may be given pretty liberally where the milk is to be sold, but must be used with caution where butter is made, or the flavour will be spoiled. Swedes should be well matured before being used for dairy cows, and this is best done by storing them early—in this situation they soon attain a ripe state. Mangel-wurzel are a much-overrated root, and are totally unfit for cows before Christmas; during March, April, May, and June they are the most nutritious. Given earlier, they are unripe, cause scour, and produce milk of poor quality, although they improve the quantity later on. They are, however, at no time rich milk-producers, being more profitable to the seller of the milk than to those who keep a dairy. The condition of the animal is almost invariably lost when these roots form a considerable portion of the food. Cow cabbage stand high in our list of foods, and not only produce excellent milk, but keep the cow in good order. The only thing against growing cabbage to a great extent, is that they come in before the grass is consumed, and therefore when keep is pretty plentiful. The carrot, however, is *the root*. It is equalled by no other, and should be grown much more largely. Sutton's long red cattle carrots, or such as are sold by other large firms, are the most profitable roots the stockowner can grow. If an animal is sick, nothing is more wholesome or more thankfully received. If the cow has a fastidious appetite, carrots prove a nutritious and tempting diet. This root is also a rich milk-producer, and gives even in winter that rich yellow colour to butter that is so much admired, and which is only otherwise obtained when cows are in the summer pasture. Carrots also keep the animal in first-class condition, and may be used nearly all the year round. The stockowner's own discretion must be used in dealing out these foods, and he should bear in mind that a mixture and change of diet is most essential. Let all possible food in winter be given in a slightly warm state—which can be arranged with the assistance of the bran mash, and by leaving the pulp and chaff twelve or eighteen hours to ferment. *A propos* of the bran mash, water should be put on at a slightly lower temperature than boiling heat, or some valuable nutritious properties are destroyed; but so long that boiling heat is not reached, these qualities are retained.

During summer, in the ordinary pastures, one cow usually requires one and a half acres to graze. No sheep or horses should be allowed in the field during summer months, although they will do good by nipping off rough grass in winter, when the cows are in the yard. Three or four lbs. of cotton-cake per head per day is not badly given even during the grass season. Ensilage is coming fast to the front, and as far as our experience goes, is especially good for dairy cows, given with hay, when no grass is forthcoming. Howbeit, the ensilage should be made of good quality of grasses or clover. It is nonsense to imagine that all weeds and innutritious herbage will make first-class ensilage.

The dairy cow should be fed at intervals, and should always clear up one serving before the next meal is given; from six until nine in the morning, hay, meals, and roots, with water, will be required; from then until the middle of the day the animal should take rest and chew the cud. At mid-day an hour or two's feeding will again be needed: most of the food to now consists of long or chopped hay and pulped roots. Towards four or five in the evening feeding must again commence, and at eight o'clock a final meal of long hay should be given with what water the animal is inclined to take. A knob of rock salt should be always in the manger. The value of manure produced by varieties of food employed is well described by Mr. Lawes, Rothamsted, as follows:—

Description of Food.	Estimated Money Value of the Manure from One Ton of each Food.		
1. Decorticated cotton-seed cake	£6	10	0
2. Rape cake	4	18	0
3. Linseed cake	4	12	0
4. Malt dust	4	5	0
5. Lentils	3	17	0
6. Linseed	3	13	0
7. Tares	3	13	6
8. Beans	3	13	6
9. Peas	3	2	6
10. Locust beans	1	2	6
11. Oats	1	14	6
12. Wheat	1	13	0
13. Indian corn	1	11	6
14. Malt	1	11	6
15. Barley	1	9	6
16. Clover hay	2	5	0
17. Meadow hay	1	10	0
18. Oat straw	0	13	6
19. Wheat straw	0	12	6
20. Barley straw	0	10	6
21. Potatoes	0	7	0
22. Mangolds	0	5	0
23. Swedish turnips	0	4	3
24. Common turnips	0	4	9
25. Carrots	0	4	0

Milking.

There are few more important things connected with the dairy than a good milkman, and there is perhaps none of the requisites so little observed by the modern cow-keepers. Here the small holder who milks his own animal has an advantage, and it is seen by his profits how much the master's interests are neglected who have to depend upon hired men. Women are the best milkers, and to women the cows will give down their milk when they would not do so to a man. The woman is gentler and kinder in all her dealings with the cow, and this animal appreciates such treatment to a high degree. The rough-handed coarse milkman, with his threatening attitude, is quite sufficient to induce the

MILKING.

cow to withhold her supply; what then must be the result when the milk-stool, the besom, or ash-plant is applied freely? The result often is that the cows frequently either go dry, prove kickers, or lose flesh, notwithstanding a liberal allowance of food; again, they abort their calves, prove fruitless, and the stock-owner finds that he is losing money by his occupation. The cow by nature only gives milk to her calf, for which she has great affection. How far then is nature lost sight of when the coarse, ill-tempered man substitutes the loved offspring!

In our numerous writings, which have extended over nearly two decades, again and again have we pointed out how much it would be to the benefit of the farmer if he would study more deeply the habits and nature of his animals, instead, as is usually the case, of treating them as mere machines rather than creatures possessing instinct and feeling in a high degree. Whether it be the horse, cow, sheep, or pig, each animal has great affection for, and fraternises with, those who show it kindness.

Assuming that a lad or maid is being instructed in milking, the first thing to advise is that the animal be driven slowly from the pasture, and as quietly as possible tied up without any ill-usage or even a hard word. When the cow walks to the shed chewing the cud, and continues doing so during milking time, the owner may know all is going well; but if, on the other hand, rumination does not go on (when no food is given), it is most likely that the animal is not well, or is in fear of the milkman. Some are of a far less nervous disposition than others, and here the attendant needs to use discretion. We always approve of a little dainty food being put to the cow during milking time, for it gives her confidence, leads her to look upon the operation with pleasure, and induces all milk to be given down readily. The teats should be wetted before milking commences, and the milker should not force the stream out more freely than the passage can take it. From too much force being used many a cow has turned out a confirmed kicker. Neither should the teats be pressed too freely until the animal opens them first, as it were, or gives the milk down; but as soon as that time comes the work should be finished with despatch. The last dregs should be taken out of the udder, as they supply the richest milk by far—the first half pint being little better than skim milk. When the animal has been milked and fed, she should be gently driven back to the pasture in summer or yard in winter time. Punctuality is a most important matter; cows should be milked to the minute at a corresponding time, night and morning. So much should this be observed, that each should be taken in its turn. When the gadfly abounds in summer, the milking-cow should be kept under a shed during the heat of the day. In milking young heifers with their first calf, much patience is needed. Often the udder is inflamed and painful, and the mother is much excited about her offspring; generally, however, in the course of a week the bag will become all right. The mother will allow the calf to take the milk, although the pain would not be endured if caused by the milkman. We never approve of lads for milking, for they are not to be depended on, and should only be employed under the eye of a good man. The master should regularly examine the

MILKING.

udders of the cows after they are milked, to ascertain if all is taken; indeed, it is a good plan to measure each cow's produce at every milking-time. Thus bad milking, inferior food, or any ailment that has attacked the cow, is at once discovered. Buckets with marks of measurement by inches can easily be obtained, thus saving the stockowner much daily trouble. Nothing proves more clearly that something is wrong with a cow than a sudden decrease in the supply.

The cow should be dried off two months at least before next calving; the milking should be stopped gradually. Once a day for a fortnight, twice a week for the next fortnight, will leave the bag so that it only occasionally needs drawing out. When an animal is a good milk-producer, the supply will not go unless the diet is given less generously, and an occasional dose of physic may be needed.

It is important that this drying-off process should be conducted with care, or a quarter of the udder may be lost at the future calving from the passage in the teats being closed.

In a lecture upon milk, delivered before the Royal Agricultural Society by Professor Voelcker, there is much matter that is interesting and instructive. On the constituent elements of milk, the Professor stated that it "was essentially an emulsion of fatty particles in solution of casine and milk-sugar. The fatty matter was not contained in it in a free condition, but was enclosed in little globules which, when the milk got sour, were precipitated. In other words, the butter and fatty portions were encased in curd or caseine. Those cells were of different sizes in different animals, and varied from $\frac{1}{10000}$th to $\frac{1}{1000}$th of an inch in diameter, some of them being round and others egg-shaped. In addition to the substances just mentioned, milk invariably contained a certain proportion of mineral matter, which consisted of the same material as the incombustible part of bone, the ash of which was rich in phosphate of lime and phosphate of magnesia. Thus bone, earth, butter, curd, milk-sugar, and mineral substances were the normal constituents of milk. In diseased milk there were a number of accidental substances which could not be identified by chemical tests, but only by the microscope. Pus generally manifested itself under the microscope in diseased milk, but even the microscope was not sufficient in all cases to prove whether milk was wholesome or not. Many things which possessed a medicinal effect were speedily absorbed into milk, and rendered often as medicinal as the original remedies; and in the same way colouring matter, such as the red of madder, the blue of indigo, or the common weeds, Mercurialis and Polygonum, passed into the milk and tinged it. The flavour of milk was sometimes materially affected by the food of the cows.

"Milk was white on account of the suspended opaque globules, and, generally speaking, the bluer it was the less cream there was in it, because the globules separated and rose to the surface; consequently, in testing milk by the eye the more opaque it was the more curd and butter it contained, and the richer it was. From September to November, generally speaking, the quality of milk became better, but it decreased in quantity; and if animals were stinted in food, not only would they yield very little, but what little they did yield would be very poor." The Professor further observed: "He had analysed the milk of the cow, the ass, the goat, ewes, and also the milk of a carnivorous animal, the dog, and it was a most singular fact that in all the various constituents of milk, and more especially in curd and butter, the milk of the dog was by far the richest. No kind of food could at all compare with it, and solid butcher-meat contained less nutritive qualities by far than did this description of milk. This would explain the difficulty of bringing up puppy dogs by hand; and, indeed, if any one wished to preserve a rare and expensive puppy that had lost its mother, the only food that could be given at all approaching in nutrition the natural food of the puppy was a very strong and concentrated effusion of beef-tea. It was also singular that naturally there was no sugar in the milk of a bitch; but after it had been domesticated and fed upon bread and starchy food it made its appearance. That showed the intimate connection between food and the composition of milk."

Disposing of the Cow.

In most instances when the cow gets past her prime she should be fatted off, sold to the London milk-dealers; or if she fails to be in calf, would be bought by the grazier. It is of little matter which course is deemed advisable to dispose of the beast; but one thing is quite certain, and that is, that the man who breeds his own stock should never have any old animals about his ground. His object should be to rear and keep the cows until they reach maturity, and then dispose of them either in high condition, coming down calving, or fatted up for the butcher. In either case, if due precaution has been taken to select good calves, to well rear and fatten, large prices will be made.

In setting about making up a cow for the butcher in summer time, little more will be needed than a good rich pasture. No other animal scarcely lays on flesh with the rapidity of a well-bred shorthorned cow that has arrived at maturity. Some of the other mentioned breeds are by no means so easily fattened, and for that reason the dairyman often prefers to sell them for what they will make as stores, thus leaving the fattening to be done by the grazier.

Stall-feeding will be the only plan in winter time, and a couple or three months will generally be sufficient to produce a ripe animal. The agents needed are good hay, swedes, cake, and meals. The animal must be lightly fed at first, and gradually brought on to its full diet. Too often the farmer hurries on his animals, giving them most injudicious quantities of food, and that of such a kind as their stomachs are unaccustomed to. Thus the cow becomes sick, refuses its food, and sometimes more serious disorders follow. Immediately the feeding cow refuses her food from being so overforced; a pint and a half of linseed oil should be given, and after an interval of two days the dose may be repeated; in the meantime, all richer food should be withheld until the patient is again in a fit state to take it. Again, a cow hurried on into condition so fast does not touch firmly, or come out well in fat when killed; this the butcher speedily detects, and buys at a low price accordingly. Stall-feeding is often found unprofitable: in many instances this loss is greatly increased by using improper diet, and by thus making the animal averse to all food.

With regard to quantity, the full-sized ox may be dieted thus: hay at all times *ad libitum*; water, ditto; sufficient roots pulped and given slightly heated to keep the bowels in a free working state; linseed cake, 3 lbs.; cotton cake, 3 lbs.; bean or pea meal, 1 gal.; rice meal, 1 gal.; sugar or treacle, 2 lbs. The above to be given each day, and to be divided into three feeds. The riper and more matured the roots are, the more freely they may be given, and the more fattening qualities they will be found to contain. There is much nonsense written about feeding animals upon certain foods which have from chemical analysis been deemed essential for hasty and profitable meat-production.

Fodder and grain vary much in their composition according to the land they are grown upon, the atmosphere and temperature they are ripened in, and the weather they are harvested in. Even Dr. Voëlcker pointed out how the public might be led astray by certain would-be scientific ones. He observes: "In speaking of the nutritive value of any article of food too precise a language is out of place; and it is simply absurd to draw general conclusions from small differences, which the analysis of different feeding materials may have yielded. Unless the differences are strongly marked and constantly observed in a great number of cases, it is unsafe and irrational to attach a precise nutritive value to different articles of food, especially if the opinion is founded solely upon analytical data, and not corroborated by actual experimental trials; for, after all, the chemical composition alone of an article of food is insufficient to determine its practical value."

Salt should be always kept in the manger of the cow in the lump state (*i.e.* rock salt), for it is essential to ensure the healthy state of the animal; and the importance of this substance in the animal economy may be learned from the fact that when the blood and other nourishing liquids in the animal system are burned, the ash which is left consists of one half its weight of common salt. Indeed, instinct appears to guide animals in their search for common salt. Thus in North America there are inland districts into which the water flows during the rainy season, and which become dry at other times, and the surface of the ground is left covered with a deposit of salt. To these districts the cattle come in herds from great distances to lick up the salt, and hence the valleys are called "Buffalo licks." Similar districts in South America, to which cattle resort, are named "Salinas."

The animal fattening in the stall needs to be kept quite quiet, and to be fed by one kind and punctual attendant. There are few men suited to the management of cattle in the fattening stages. This class are commonly found to be both careless and indolent, men looking forward only to pay-night, and caring no more for the animals under their care than the stone walls which surround them. Then there are those who out of kindness over-feed and keep the manger too full. The valuable man is one who knows to a nicety the amount of food each cow requires, feeds them accordingly, and avoids above all any waste. A quantity of food remaining in the manger is as distasteful to the lower animals as to the human being would be a joint never removed from his presence.

The Dairy.

In the first place, for the sake of coolness, the building used for the dairy should have a northern aspect, to get as little of the sun as possible, or it must be shaded in some way. It is preferable if the rooms used for storing the milk be a few feet below the level of the ground, a more suitable atmosphere being so obtained. It is essentially necessary that everything connected with a dairy room, utensils, and attendants be kept perfectly clean. Milk and butter are most susceptible to taints from any impurities in utensils or the air; for which last reason the dairy should be far removed from piggeries or anything emitting offensive effluvia. Stone or slate shelves are best. The leaden or earthenware milk pans should be shallow, from four to six inches deep, as milk thin set keeps better than when in deeper vessels; and though it may be preserved longer in winter than in summer, we would not even then recommend pans being used deeper than six inches. Before being milked cows should on no account be hurried so as to overheat them; hence, in summer, the shorter distance they have to travel home the better; and in the pastures where they lie there should be some trees or other shelter from the sun, as overheated milk will not keep so well.

When brought into the dairy, the milk should be allowed to cool a little before it is poured through a fine strainer into the pans in which it is to set for cream. The cream should be taken off only once in twenty-four hours instead of every twelve hours, as is commonly done in small dairies; the reason being that the oftener the milk is skimmed the more milk is taken up with the cream, giving it a tendency to become sour soon, as cream keeps longer fresh than milk. To insure really good butter, cream should not be kept in summer longer than four days, or a week in cold weather is the most we would recommend.

In winter, before putting the cream into the churn, the latter should be warmed a little. This requires careful management, or sometimes a man may be churning half a day in severe weather before the butter comes. If possible, the cream in the churn should be at the same temperature summer and winter. Where circular churns are used, they should be turned slowly at first, gradually increasing the pace till the butter is formed, which should be in about an hour. The churn requires turning much faster in winter than in summer.

When taken from the churn, the butter should be well washed in cold water, salted according to requirements, and made up. After this it should be kept dry. It is a mistake many people make to place butter in water during hot weather. It keeps much better quite dry in a cool atmosphere. When sent to market it should be wrapped in dry cloths.

To turn out first-class butter requires some experience on the part of the dairymaid; but attention to cleanliness and the thorough washing of the butter are points not to be overlooked. The buttermilk, *i.e.* the milk left after churning, is used for pigs; and the milk, after being skimmed, can be given to calves or pigs. Where new milk is sent to market a great deal of trouble is saved in the dairy, the cows only requiring to be milked regularly, and the milk cooled before being despatched. To expedite the latter, when time is limited, an apparatus is used in large establishments—the milk being passed through tubes round which cold water is forced; immediately after which it may be forwarded to market or railway station. Should the milk be sent off before cooling, and confined in air-tight tins, it would not only taste disagreeably, but would keep badly.

The dairy should be well ventilated. It should be built so that a cool temperature in summer and a warm one in winter can be insured. Shady trees and low-growing shrubs are advised in the vicinity, but not so near as to droop upon the building.

On the requisites to be attended to in the construction of dairies, the following *resumé* of points, detailed in a report from the pen of the late lamented Prince Albert, will be of interest. They comprise nearly all the points to be attended to, and were carried out in the Royal Farm at Windsor :—" Air was to circulate freely round the dairy; shelter was to be had from the south and west; trees were to be excluded from close contact with it, none nearer than thirty feet, and all neighbouring shrubs to be close standards. The soil, if possible, a gravel subsoil; ample ventilation to be secured within the building both at top and at its sides; windows to be double, to secure warmth in winter, cold in summer; water to be plentifully supplied; means for rapidly flushing the drains ; no cesspools to be near the building; the walls to be hollow ; the roof such as that no vicissitudes of weather should affect the milk; the floors and walls to be paved and covered with glazed tiles; the tables and shelves of marble or of slate."

A thatched roof tiled over for neatness will give the most uniform temperature winter and summer.

The creamers, where used in the dairy, will be likely to cause a complete revolution in the arrangements. They are especially suited for those whose business it is to make use of the skim milk for either selling, calf-rearing, or even for pigs. Our own particular experience has been with Coolley's creamer — an American invention (manufactured by Messrs. Lloyd Lawrence & Co., 34 Worship Street, Finsbury, London) —and we can strongly recommend it to our readers.

Mr. W. Coolley, of Washington County, Vermont, has imposed a debt of gratitude upon the public for his discovery, which he introduced in 1876, although it has only lately become known in England, but will doubtless in a short space of time become in regular use. The invention has taken gold medals in Pennsylvania, New York, Paris, and London, and many other places. A prejudice still exists amongst some of the old school of dairy people; but having had the apparatus under our own eyes, we can sufficiently vouch for its suitability for the dairyman with one or two cows, also for the possessor of the comparatively large herd, always providing that a fair supply of water of a temperature between 45° and 52° Fahrenheit is at hand.

The following description, with above illustration, will give a clear idea to our readers of the simplicity of the invention :—

Fig. 1 shows this portable vessel containing fou. tins, but it can be made to hold more. This refrigerator, or creamer, is filled with water, and the tins are submerged, while to keep them under water will be noticed four strips of wood fixed across the creamer.

Fig. 2 exhibits a magnified tin taken from the water. "A" is the lid; "B" is glass fixed in the tin, which shows the cream as it rises, and can either

Fig. 1.—The Portable Creamer holding Four Tins.

be ordered in the tin or not, as it is more for curiosity than use; "C" is a second glass, which is very requisite to observe when the milk is run off and only cream remains: "D" is the tap that draws off the milk; and "E" shows the distance that the handle of the tap should be turned to prevent the cream running off with the milk.

Fig. 3 presents a tin submerged in water; the position of water, air, cream, and milk is here clearly defined.

We will now relate some of the advantages of the creamer. First, the new milk being placed in water the temperature as above described, the whole of the

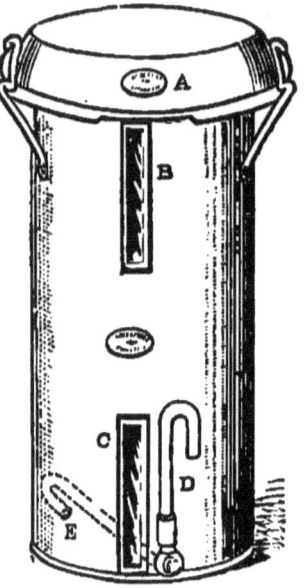 

Fig. 2.—One of the Tins Magnified.   Fig. 3.—A Tin Submerged in Water.

cream rises in twelve hours; and if the water stands at a still lower temperature, the cream rises in a corresponding shorter time. The great advantage of securing the cream so quickly, as in the space of twelve hours in the heat of summer, is great indeed. It is the cry throughout the land in the sultry weather,

THE FARMER'S VETERINARY ADVISER:
A Guide to the Prevention and Treatment of Disease in Domestic Animals.

By JAMES LAW,
Fellow of the Royal College of Veterinary Surgeons of Great Britain;
Author of "General and Descriptive Anatomy of Domestic Animals."

In One 8vo Volume, with numerous Illustrations, cloth, price 12s. 6d.

"In this 'Adviser' we find everything necessary to be known by the amateur of the more common, and even some of the rarer, forms of disease, as well as the accidents to which quadrupeds and poultry are liable—the whole being brought up to the most advanced standard of veterinary science. We know of no work on the subject in any language which, in the same space, embraces so much. While the technicalities of science are interpreted in words which must be intelligible to the meanest understanding, and the whole book is written in a terse attractive style, nothing is omitted which pertains to the most recent investigations and discoveries. We certainly have no other book like this."—*The Veterinary Journal, London.*

"The diseases of all our domesticated animals, and the more important ones of poultry, are described, and most approved treatment given. I have no hesitation in saying that this is *the most useful and therefore the best* work on the diseases of animals in the English language. It is wonderful how much information has been compressed within the limits of a small volume. Before the publication of this work a farmer was obliged to purchase a small library to have at command advice on different diseases to which his animals are liable, and even then it could not always be relied on. The treatment is particularly complete."—*Country Gentleman.*

THE COW AND CALF:
A Practical Manual on the Cow and Calf in Health and Disease.

By JOHN WALKER,
Author of "How to Farm with Profit."

In crown 8vo, price 1s. 6d.

The primary object of this book is to define each subject, so as to render it comprehensible alike to the amateur as also to the proficient agriculturist.

From the unprofitableness of crop-raising in this country, it is becoming evident that it is to the *animals* of the farm that those must look for support whose daily bread depends upon the products of their lands.

"Well calculated to instruct the novice, and to assist the experienced."—*Land and Water.*

By the Same Author.

THE GADFLY OF THE OX (*Œstrus Bovis*).
Their History, Life, Prevention, Destruction; and Losses sustained thereby, computed at £2,474,195 annually in Great Britain.

Price Sixpence.

LONDON: THOMAS C. JACK, 45 LUDGATE HILL.
EDINBURGH : GRANGE PUBLISHING WORKS.

OUR DOMESTIC ANIMALS
In Health and Disease.
BY JOHN GAMGEE,
Late Principal of the New Veterinary College, Edinburgh.

In Four Volumes, crown 8vo, price £1. 4s., cloth. Also in Twenty Parts at 1s. each.

THE GREAT AUK, OR GAREFOWL:
Its History, Archæology, and Remains.
BY SYMINGTON GRIEVE,
EDINBURGH.

Illustrated, in a Handsome 4to Volume, price 15s., cloth.

THE HENWIFE:
Her Own Experience in Her Own Poultry-Yard.
BY THE HON. MRS ARBUTHNOTT.

In One crown 8vo Volume, Illustrated with Ten Fine Plates of Poultry by HARRISON WEIR, price 3s. 6d. Cheap Edition, 1s. 6d.

This is one of the most popular, favourite, and useful Poultry Books, the Authoress having for many years been a most successful rearer and exhibitor of all kinds of Poultry.

The following subjects are treated in the Volume:—Houses and Yards—Food—Hatching—Chickens and Ducklings—Exhibition—Diseases and Remedies—Fattening—Summer Management—Preserving and Sale of Eggs—and a full description of the Points of all the varieties of Poultry.

THE TAXIDERMIST'S MANUAL;
Or the Art of Preserving Objects of Natural History.
BY CAPTAIN THOMAS BROWN, F.L.S., &c.,

Crown 8vo, cloth, price 2s. 6d., Illustrated.

A Description of the various IMPLEMENTS required in making collections of Plants and Animals intended to be preserved; with Directions how to use them.

LONDON: THOMAS C. JACK, 45 LUDGATE HILL.
EDINBURGH: GRANGE PUBLISHING WORKS.

THE DAIRY.

when thunder is in the air, that the milk goes sour before half the cream can be taken under the old system. The milk, which should be fresh and wholesome for calves, or such like, is sour and unfit for use, and if administered to young animals, likely enough causes scour or more serious ills.

Where the creamer is used no loss is here sustained, therefore not only is much more butter made, but the skim milk is as wholesome as in winter.

Second, much less dairy room is needed. No long rows of shelves for milk vessels are required. The apparatus may be placed in the garden, orchard, or any out-buildings where the water supply is laid on. It is better that it should be under cover, particularly in winter, or in unpropitious weather, for then it would be unpleasant work taking the milk and cream away and setting the new milk, although the operation would only last a few minutes. Third, the saving of labour is a feature not to be overlooked in these days when it is most difficult to obtain servants who will conscientiously attend to such matters. Indeed a tolerable milkman can, with a little care, do in a few minutes all that is required when the creamer is brought into use. Only the tins need to be cleaned, and as they are continually in use, and hold four gallons each, not many of these are required. They can be made to hold more or less, but four gallons is the usual size. When the evening meal comes in, the morning one is removed, and the same tins used. The same process as in the morning is gone through at this, the evening meal.

Fourth, more butter is made from a certain quantity of cream by about half a pound to the ordinary cow, and this may be reckoned on for the summer months.

It might appear to some of our readers that still extra cream may be obtained by allowing the milk to stand over the twelve hours, but such is not the case if the water is of a sufficiently cold temperature. To prove this we submerged a tin for a second twelve hours, but no cream worth mentioning came to the top. The inventor claims that the creamer tends to produce better butter, seeing that the milk does not become contaminated by impurities of the atmosphere, the odours, gases ; the taints of turnips and artificial foods in the milk are effectually disposed of. Reasonable as this may appear, we have been unable as yet to try experiments upon this point, so cannot substantiate or condemn the inventor's opinion. Fifth, it is much cheaper than working the butter in the ordinary manner, no other vessels being needed except a cream tin and churn, and thus much expense is avoided.

Supposing a person to have but a small dairy, and to be desirous of trying this plan upon an economical basis, he can use any old beer-barrel, chest, or even build a cistern at less expense than the apparatus costs that holds the tins ; these answer just as well so long as the tins are totally submerged in water. To beginners in dairying, who have to buy all utensils, this new system is more particularly suited. An ordinary thirty-six-gallon barrel will hold two full-sized tins of four gallons, for they only measure twenty inches in depth, and eight and a half in diameter.

Sixth, we estimate that all calves, reared from this new system of managing the milk, average, when twelve months old, a pound more per head in value. Where calves are reared in the hot summer months, farmers are put well nigh to their wits' end to arrange provision for them. The milk is at certain times *all* sour, and if some of the artificial foods, which now are so easily to be procured, were not at hand, the poor thirsty calves would fare badly indeed. Some resort to new milk for the calves, seeing the skimmed is sour: but here the weekly butter supply is curtailed, and the purchaser is disappointed at not having his usual supply. The new system of setting milk guards against such casualties.

We now come to the most important point, viz., the water supply. As we have before observed, the temperature must not be warmer than $53°$, and the more below such a temperature the sooner the cream rises. So it happens in the dull, dark days of midwinter, when it is not convenient to milk exactly at a corresponding time night and morning, that the cream has already risen, although the meals of the day are only divided by about ten hours. At a temperature of $32°$ the cream would all rise in eight or nine hours. It is advisable to let the water run through the creamer for the first half-hour if practicable, as the warmth from the milk and tin raises the temperature of the water considerably. It is not so difficult to arrange the water supply as at first might be imagined, for from pretty well every homestead a single pipe can be laid to some distant or adjacent hill. Not very much water is really needed. The tins of new milk can be cooled in the previous water, and, if cold enough, this water can be utilised a second and third time, for it is perfectly clean. By letting a trickling stream run through the creamer, the warmer water is quickly removed, for it must be understood the latter always floats to the surface, and therefore is easily run off.

We trust, then, that with such a useful discovery as the Cooley Creamer, ensilage, and other such ingenious inventions, that the British farmer may retrieve some of the heavy losses he has lately sustained from disease among his herds and flocks, untoward seasons, foreign competition, and high price of labour. It is only reasonable to expect new and more useful inventions will be found out with regard to the dairy, rearing, and fattening processes, for here alone profit can at present be made. English agriculturists are fully alive to the fact that to traverse the old ruts leads to ruin, and it is regretable to conjecture how numerous have been the victims who have passed the paths of sorrow during the last half-dozen years. Let the young and enterprising farmer bestir himself in these matters. It is more and more clearly defined that England must become a pastoral country, that her fort must be rearing and fattening herds and flocks and selling dairy productions, for these are the agricultural industries now most suited to our lands. Just as the foreigner has defeated the Englishman in his own market in grain, so may the British farmer challenge the world to compete with him in the meat market so long as the home grazier will set about his work in an approved manner, and make use of every useful invention.

What of the arable land ? The sooner such as can be converted into pasture is thus transformed the better, and the plough must be cast into the ditch. Thus the old lines of an esteemed poet will need reversing—

"The first creditor in every state is the plough."

It is sad to contemplate that for the last decade in England it has been a debtor of great magnitude.

Treatment of the Calf.

It should be engrafted on the mind of the breeder that to rear a profitable and creditable animal he must begin at birth, and generous but discreet treatment must be continued until the animal is matured. Few animals find their way into a showyard that have not been treated well from their earliest days, fewer still carry off honours. A large percentage of the animals bred are neglected in the first fortnight of their existence, not a few die from bad management, and not one in twenty is so reared as to maintain its calf's flesh. If ever this flesh is lost it is never regained, and twelve months are lost in the fattening process of the animal.

No sooner does poverty display itself in the young animal than disease, finding the gates open for its attack, steps in ; and if a true return could be given of calves that never survive the first year, it would astonish every breeder.

We observed above that a year was lost when the calve's flesh was allowed to fall off; and we aver that a young beast that has not lost its early flesh will come out worth as much at two and a half years old as the neglected one will at three years and a half. Nothing ensures this generous rearing so much as letting the offspring run with the cow, and this is a common practice with Hereford breeders, and has doubtless much to do with the excellent white-faced bullocks we see got up for our Christmas markets.

Howbeit, it is too expensive for the ordinary breeder

of good bred beasts to allow the calf to take all the milk, and therefore more economical means must be used. Many a time, however, the writer has reared a couple of calves upon a Welsh cow or some animal not too valuable; and one cow will rear two calves better than they can be reared with the bucket if the cream is taken off the milk. When this method is attempted, however, it should be on the summer pasture, and calves reared in this manner may afterwards be identified by a stranger among any number brought up in the ordinary way, being so much better developed.

A few remarks upon calves' foods is essential. The leading dealers (Messrs. Bibby & Son, and others) give some excellent substitutes for milk; few breeders of cattle fail to find the use of some kind in cases of emergency most useful and even necessary; but often the feeds are but substitutes, and do not prove in any way as nutritious as the mother's milk. Still where the latter runs short, we advise free use of such feeds; for liberal treatment the young animals must have. The calf-feeds do not frequently receive proper care from the farmer and his servants, thus the seller scarcely gets his dues; and so it comes to pass that while one man's herd of calves looks excellent upon some bought diet, his neighbour's have a very indifferent appearance. In many instances, doubtless, such a state may be traced to carelessness on the part of the servant in preparing the food. Indeed, the same fault is observable in supplying the mother's milk. Food given to calves a little too warm or a little too cold may bring on scour or other disorders that may be either of trivial consequence or may lead to death; and seeing how difficult it is at the present day to get reliable servants for *ordinary* domestic work, it may be considered tenfold more so to find agents for the most responsible of all offices, viz., that of calf-rearing and general attendance upon young animals. The fact is, that the master's eye and the master's hand alone will guarantee careful attention.

We will now commence with the treatment of the calf at birth. Assuming that the mother has a comfortable bed, the calf can be left for a few hours after birth, and upon next visiting the shed it must be ascertained if it has taken any milk. The herdsman will form a good opinion about this by examining the udder of the cow. If the young animal has helped itself, well; but if not, it must be assisted to do so. When it has once sucked, no further fear need be felt on this head. It should be allowed to enjoy the mother's milk and company for a week; the practice of removing the youngster immediately after birth should be discouraged, if its future welfare is to be studied. Aside from the mother's bag being reduced considerably and more naturally by the calf, the rich milk or colostrum that the mother gives the first few days acts as a slight purge upon the bowels and clears offensive matter from the intestines, leaving them in healthy working order. When the calf is removed from the cow at birth it has not the advantage of the beastling, or colostrum, or first milk, and in consequence becomes in not a few cases costive, and this costiveness generally, later on, leads to the opposite evil, diarrhœa; this is hard to cure, and when remedied the young creature looks an abject thing indeed. The uneducated cattle-breeder "gangs his ane gait." He removes the calf at birth, and as a substitute for its mother's milk gives some new milk perhaps from a cow that has been milked some time, and which contains scarcely an atom of the colostrum so needful to prevent constipation so frequently followed on by acid secretions on the lining membranes of the intestines. These acid secretions coagulate the milk and separate into component parts; the curd or cheesy part remains as a foreign or irritating agent in the intestines, and the fluid or *whey* part comes away in the form of semi-fluid fæces. This disease is above all things to be avoided in calves, and goes by the name of gastroenteritis or white scour. To prevent such a complaint the ignorant breeder gives the young calf doses of some purging medicine such as castor-oil — this is perhaps the best thing he could give under the circumstances, but avails little while milk of inferior quality is still supplied to so tender a stomach; others give medicine to cause costiveness, and this is much to be condemned. The fact is, nature's laws are being abruptly broken, and in animals so young results are sure to be unsatisfactory. Therefore we do not advise that the calf should be weaned from the cow until a week old, when its intestines will be in a state to receive food of a less delicate character. The calf, when removed, should be placed out of hearing of the cow in a dry, warm, but well-ventilated shed, and a good bed of straw is most essential.

We now put the calf upon three meals per day, each meal to consist of three pints of milk. Not such as has been robbed of the cream, neither necessarily very rich new milk, but just such as is of fair quality. This treatment may continue until the animal is one month old. At this age calves are too often supposed to only require milk of the thinnest character, such as has been skimmed "sky blue," and has not the needful nutritious qualities in it. In some instances, questionable messes are added to the milk, boiled linseed is frequently used, but not being cooked discreetly gives but an unsatisfactory result. Here some well-prepared advertised calf food had far better be used. Howbeit, those who cannot spare milk of good quality should not attempt to rear, and breeders must at times be content to put up with less butter in the calf-rearing establishment.

From one to three months old give the calf three quarts of milk each end of the day, and the cream may be taken from it once. The animal will now begin to pick a little sweet hay, and for economy's sake a small coarse net should be placed filled with the fodder near the head. Hay is little given unchopped at this time, although later on the small trough may be introduced, and a little linseed-cake dust and some pulped carrots or swedes be supplied. It is most essential that the hay and all other food given at this time should be of the best quality, for the digestive powers of the young animals at this age are by no means strong, and are all unaccustomed to the work required of them. The hay that is got without exposure to rain, in June, is the best for calves, providing it has not been allowed to heat in the rick. We like to see it come out the same colour as it goes in, and to contain the same sweet aroma. Hay got later on is too woody in the stems, and indigestible for calves, and is often the cause of several common ills to which calves are subject.

From three to six months old the quantity of milk

may be increased and the quality reduced. The hay and roots should be increased, but up till twelve months old, cotton cake must be carefully withheld. The latter is too indigestible for calves—portions passing through them whole, thus causing purging, irritation of the stomach and bowels. Carrots may be looked upon as the most wholesome root, and mangel-wurzel as the least wholesome. Cow cabbages are very good when they can be obtained, and swedes are advised when the young animals get strong enough to digest them. A little linseed cake, rice meal, pea or bran meal, or wheaten meal, are each wholesome when given prudently and moderately.

In rearing calves with the bucket, it is very essential that the animals should be all tied separately before they are fed, and if left tied for a quarter of an hour afterwards they will not acquire the much-detested habit of sucking each other. Moreover, when tied, each animal gets its share of milk, without being subjected to the blows frequently administered by the unfeeling attendant in order to keep one calf from interfering with its companion's food.

After six months old the milk can be entirely withheld; indeed it should be rendered of very poor quality during the last month, then it is not so much missed. Until twelve months old, light and wholesome food is the proper diet, and the judicious stockmaster will judge what kind is suitable, according to the thriving or otherwise of his stock. Chopped hay, and sweet straw mixed with pulped roots, and laid by to ferment, will form the standing diet for yearlings. The young animals will then be easily treated by any ordinary herdsman, and may be considered safely

TREATMENT OF THE CALF.

reared. With regard to water, that termed soft, or rain water, is preferable.

Our above advice has chiefly pointed to the winter season, howbeit even in summer calves should not be turned to grass too young. It may be taken as sound counsel not to allow them to be depastured while they are taking milk, for grass and milk do not go well together. There is no objection to a little green vegetable mixed with chopped hay, but they should not be offered otherwise.

Michaelmas is a good time to bring calves in for rearing, and then they go to pasture in May straight from milk. Many rearers will not allow their youngsters to go to grass before twelve months old, and such rearers can often show the best herds of cattle.

Only full-sized and healthy-looking calves should be chosen for rearing. Any not reaching the standard should be fattened for the butcher. They are fatted best by being kept confined, and the mother being allowed to visit them twice a-day, or by being given a full supply of new milk of the best quality.

The milk-seller usually finds it best to dispose of his calves to the highest bidder soon after their birth, for it is his business to find the maximum quantity of milk for the market, and these young animals are a minor consideration.

By paying attention to the above simple matters with regard to calf-rearing, the occupation will be found a profitable one, but without heed to minute details in management, the stockmaster will only reap disappointment.

Diseases of Animals.

There are few matters associated with stock where farmers are more at fault than in the treatment and prevention of diseases in the animals under their care; and, looking upon the thing both in a pecuniary and humane light, it behoves them to more deeply contemplate their ignorance. Without diving far into the veterinary art it is quite practicable for the stockowner to treat the cow and calf in some of the common ailments, and it is within his power alone to use preventive means.

Such plain instructions, then, shall be given here that may be practised by the ordinary stockowner, while any more intricate maladies we leave in the hands of properly qualified veterinary surgeons—most easily obtainable—while the empiric is dispensed with altogether. The veterinary chemist is to be found in every town who is ever ready to mix up the required medicines, and also to advise the farmer how to administer the potion.

Abortion.

This is the disorder from which the breeder suffers greater loss than from any other, and it more commonly arises from the following causes:—

1. *Unwholesome Food.*
2. *Unwholesome Water.*
3. *Ill-treatment.*
4. *Sympathy.*
5. *Fright.*

Unwholesome Food.

Amongst common causes the following food may be classed as being productive of the disorder. Hay that is over-ripened in the field becomes of a woody indigestible character, innutritious and unwholesome to a degree. Hay badly harvested or overheated in the stack is little better ; and we do not counsel too much chopped food, for occasionally the knots in the straw or hay cause colic. This latter evil may, however, be to a certain extent obviated by the chopped food being blended with pulped roots and being mixed from twelve to twenty-four hours before being used, during which time the knots in the straw or hay become softened. Sometimes in the spring season pregnant cows are allowed to feed upon old grass, or " fog ; " but this is injudicious, for at such a time they often feed with avidity upon any vegetable diet, and such unwholesome herbage has been found to cause much mischief. Again, grass with frost on it is likely to have an evil effect. Ergot in grasses—of which we have spoken in another part of this book —is one of the most fruitful causes of "slinking" amongst cows, while hard tough swedes grown on poor soil are indigestible, and also mangel wurzel too early in the season. Still, roots of good quality are strongly recommended.

Unwholesome Water.

The filthy ponds, muddy rivers and their tributaries, liberally mixed with excretion and urine from the very animals which seek the stream to quench their daily thirst, is another common cause, while cold spring water given too liberally when the animals are thirsty is to be condemned. Rain water or spring water tempered in the sun or a warm temperature, is to be advised. In certain instances springs strongly impregnated with iron have been known to cause whole herds to abort. The above are simple matters, and within the farmer's power to correct.

Ill-treatment.

Abuse from herdsmen of evil dispositions, over-driving, chasing with dogs, abuse or over-haste in driving to and from the milking, sheds, and malicious treatment while milking, are acts strongly condemned, for thus the nervous system is upset, and the worst results may be apprehended. Again, ill-treatment at the fairs and over-driving to and from the sale-ground should be avoided. To deprive cows too long of water or food is a common practice of the drover, and as often causes some mischief.

Sympathy.

How far sympathy, or what is commonly called infection from another cow that has given an untimely birth, can be assigned a cause, is yet doubtful. Neither medical men nor stockowners are settled upon this point, and for our own part we, as a rule, attribute such cases as are supposed to emanate from sympathy to the unwholesome food or water that all animals in a herd are liable or compelled to partake of alike—hence the same general result. Still, lest peradventure sympathy really was a cause, it is wise to remove the cow that brings forth at undue time, and also to carefully remove and disinfect any aborted remains. If the herdsman is worthy of his situation he will detect symptoms several days before the birth takes place, and remove the cow from the herd accordingly. Again, if a cow has once done amiss it is unwise to keep her on to breed from again, or the same mistake is likely to be made.

Fright.

Pregnant cows should be guarded from fright. A pack of hounds, a brace of pointers, an unruly sheep-dog, or the prowling cur that makes nocturnal visits to or through the herd, are liable to cause much mischief to an animal so nervous as the cow, and one that is more subject to abortion than any other. Sudden disturbances, such as heavy thunder and vivid lightning, not unusually are attended with evil, therefore it behoves the stock-keeper to keep his animals as quiet and undisturbed as possible.

The above is one of the maladies that the farmer or even the veterinary surgeon has but little chance of treating with success, for usually in spite of every precaution the first symptoms are followed on pretty quickly by such others that portray pretty clearly that an untimely birth will shortly transpire. We trust, however, to have defined the means of prevention by removing causes, which are in the hands of every farmer and grazier, and these are preferable to cure.

Foot-and-Mouth Disease.
(*Eczema Epizootica.*)

This, an important disease, first visited Great Britain in 1839, and then fatal results were common. Howbeit, although the malady has visited us since at intervals, yet it has ever assumed a more mild form. Under present restrictions it is to be hoped outbreaks will be at once stamped out, and what is more to the purpose, that it will not be allowed to pass our guards on the sea-coast. Farmers were slow at being convinced that the malady was not indigenous to our land; but the strong measures used in the last large outbreak have been responded to, and all best-informed people now allow that not only is the disease an imported one, but that it is spread by contagion, and contagion alone.

Symptoms.—The germs of the disease are from three to ten days developing themselves in the system. In the early stages the animal will be isolated from the herd, walk with a stiff gait, while a discharge of saliva will be observed to flow from the mouth. In the milder attacks no more strong marks of illness will be noticed, but if a more malignant form sets in great lameness will follow on, often accompanied with such soreness of the mouth that the poor animals, although wishing to eat, dare not satisfy the desire, because of the pain caused by so doing. Sometimes the disease begins in the feet, and the lameness and ulcerated state of the space between the hoof is very great, the mouth at the same time not being so much affected. In other cases the mouth suffers more severely, and in worst attacks of all, both the feet and mouth are in a most painful state. The attack is ushered in by fever, heat of the mouth, the lining of the mouth of an unnatural pink colour, attended with a flow of ropy saliva, which flows in a fine string. Rumination ceases, the animal is unable to graze, making a mumbling ineffective effort. The udder is inflamed and painful to the touch; vesicles or small blisters cover the tongue, roof of the mouth, and lip, varying in size from a threepenny piece to a shilling. The vesicles are found on the coronets between the claws, and the hoof is hot and tender. The vesicles in the mouth are similar to such as are raised with a hot iron, and contain a transparent fluid. In the dairy cow the milk is suspended, and on the teats the vesicles so abound as to make the act of milking a most painful operation, the blisters being broken with every pressure of the teats. Constipation is nearly always observed. In still more malignant cases large pieces of the lining membrane slough off from the inside of the mouth, the tongue is swollen to so large a size as to prevent the suffering patient from getting it inside. In the feet the vesicles form into ulcers, and discharge a sanious fœtid matter. The internal organs suffer, and gangrene of the lungs or some other fatal organ ensues, until at last death releases the suffering patient. The most marked symptom of the disease, and one that displays itself in an early stage, is a peculiar smacking sound which the animal makes with its tongue and lips from the former sticking to the roof of the mouth.

Treatment.—In by far the majority of cases the patient needs little treatment. The disease being so very contagious, the animal should be isolated, and in winter put into a warm but well-ventilated box. To relieve the costiveness 1 lb. of Epsom salts may be given with an ounce of ground ginger. The food must consist of such dry soft diet as the animal can take with its inflamed mouth. Bran mashes, with softened linseed cake, pulped carrots, and such like, feed well, but chaff and hay is too hard for the inflammatory state of the mouth. The water should be slightly chilled, and a liberal supply given. Clean dry straw for litter is the best. The manure should be constantly removed, and the feet should be kept clean. Such plain treatment will be all that is needed in winter time; while in summer, when the animal is at grass, mild cases may well be left to themselves. In more intricate cases it is well to call in a veterinary surgeon, who will examine the mouth, and, if the vesicles are broken and ulcers formed, will probably apply a little cooling lotion mixed as follows: Alum, half an ounce; water, one pint. The mouth should be sponged out with this once or twice a day. Another excellent lotion may be made by dissolving sixty grains of permanganate of potass in one pint of water, and using in a like manner. When the animal fails to eat, it should be drenched with some good gruel two or three times a day, in which may be mingled a little good ale.

Prevention.—Let the herdsman who attends upon the sick cattle keep clear of healthy animals. Let all the manure be removed and burnt or disinfected. Let the milk from dairy cows be carefully put aside, for it has been known to carry the disease to calves, pigs, and even to human beings. Lastly, let the stockowner treat the disorder in every way as the most contagious one to which our stock is subject, for such it certainly is.

Hoven or Blown.

(*Tympanitis.*)

Hoven is the natural distension of the rumen or paunch with gaseous fluids, caused by the natural peristaltic action of the stomach being suspended, hence the elimination of gaseous matter from the accumulated ingesta.

The writer has found it of common occurrence in the spring months, when the grass is fresh, plentiful, and full of rich juicy matter. Care should be taken in stocking fields of grass at this season, where rank herbage abounds, and also in depasturing stock in clovers, or feeding with artificial grasses, lucerne, vetches, &c. Although the complaint is not often attended with serious results, yet cattle have been sometimes found in early morning, in spring-time, dying from suffocation, shortly after taking their too hearty breakfast. We find the hoar-frosts, which generally prevail at spring-time, rain, or even heavy dews, cause the grasses to become more indigestible, and on such mornings in certain pastures the shepherd not uncommonly finds one or more of the herd suffering.

Symptoms.—The higher part of the left side swells up, sometimes quickly, sometimes slowly, and in some cases both right and left side expand until the swellings are elevated above the back. Rumination ceases, the animal is in great pain, moans, stretches out its neck, husks or coughs with the vain endeavour to eject wind, respiration becomes laboured, the nostrils are distended, there is grinding of the teeth, and the pulse is imperceptible. In the malignant cases, as the animal gets worse it bellows, stamps with its feet, its back becomes arched and stiff, its eyes grow dim, it staggers, falls down, and dies in convulsions, a greenish foamy liquid coming from the mouth and nose. In some cases hoven takes a chronic form, and each morning the animal will be found blown up on one side, although not sufficiently so to cause illness; and later on, when the pasture becomes dry, the symptoms will have all disappeared.

Treatment.—The diet of the animal subject to attacks must be attended to. If lying on the too luxuriant pasture, the cow should be removed at night, and given some dry food such as hay, and should not be allowed to return to the pasture until the herbage is dry. When cattle are first depastured upon any luxuriant herbage, they should only be allowed to feed a few hours at a time, until they become accustomed to their new food. In bad attacks Murray advises that the animal's head should be elevated on a line with its neck, and a probang passed down the gullet into the rumen, from which the gas will escape with a hiss. Still the indigestible agent needs removing; and we have ourselves found either linseed oil in 1½ to 2-pint doses, or 1 lb. of Epsom salts and 2 ounces of ground ginger, generally give relief. When animals have once been blown, they are more subject to disease in the future, and they should be carefully dieted after the attack.

When the chronic state of the disease is assumed, 1½ pints of linseed oil should be given to relieve, and as a tonic and stimulant the following:—

Powdered gentian . . . . . 4 drachms.
Powdered ginger . . . . . . 4 do.
Linseed meal . . . . . . 2 do.

To be given twice a-day in a quart of warm ale.

In serious cases the rumen has to be pierced, and the proper spot operated on. It is one hand's-breadth from the projection of the hip, and the same breadth from the last rib on the left side. An instrument called a trocar is used; but is only advised to be applied in the hands of the qualified veterinary surgeon.

Engorgement of the Rumen.

(*Grain Sick.*)

This is a disease similar to hoven or blown, but often of a more serious nature. It is called "grain sick" from milking cows frequently suffering in London and other large towns from eating too many grains. Other foods are liable to cause the disorder, such as too much meal, &c.

Symptoms.—The rumen is enlarged as in hoven, but instead of feeling hollow and drum-like, as does the rumen in that complaint, the paunch has a soft doughy feeling, and when pressed the impression of the hand "pits," *i.e.*, will be left for some time after the hand is removed. The animal is dull, rumination ceases, appetite is lost, and the respiration is at first slightly affected, and still more so as the malady becomes more declared. The pulse is not much affected, and constipation is usually observed. Dobson writes:—

The treatment is of course to get rid of the contents of the rumen as speedily as possible; and first of all a brisk cathartic, combined with a stimulant, ought to be given.

Epsom salts	12 to 18 ounces.
Powdered ginger	1 ounce.
Aromatic spirit of ammonia	1 ounce.
Solution of aloes	4 ounces.

Given in a large quantity of warm gruel or ale. This may be followed up with repeated doses of linseed oil every few hours, till an action on the bowels is perceived; and the dose itself repeated in twelve hours if no relief is obtained. The animal's left side, over the region of the rumen, should be well rubbed with the hand, and a certain amount of exercise given.

For a long time after the animal has recovered the grain diet must not be resumed, for the coats of the rumen have been over-disturbed, and must not again be taxed until they are in a sound healthy state.

Catarrh or Cold.

This disorder most commonly occurs in the spring season when animals are first depastured. About this time, before the hedges have burst forth into foliage, and yet while the cow has already assumed her fine summer garment, the penetrating east wind, which more often than not prevails at such a season in this country, brings on catarrh. Again, it arises from cattle being kept in too warm sheds at night, and being exposed by day. This ailment is not dangerous of itself, although the animals themselves exhibit well-defined symptoms of constitutional disturbance which call for immediate attention, or a graver aspect of the disorder will be assumed.

Symptoms.—The animal will be separated from the herd; shivering fits will come on at intervals; defluxion of mucus from the nostrils will be observed, and also a stiffness of gait with slight fever. Later on is seen a dry nostril, accelerated pulse, and cessation of rumination. The latter symptom is an undeniable proof that something is amiss with the bovine species.

Treatment.—The animal should be at once removed to a loose but airy box without draught. Food must consist of bran mashes wherein a little fresh salt is sprinkled, a few pulped carrots, and some sweet hay. The bowels are usually costive, and to relieve these give

  Epsom salts . . . . . . 12 ounces.
  Ground ginger . . . . . . ¾ ounce.

These ingredients to be mixed in a quart of warm ale. The animal should have chilled water, wherein half an ounce of nitre is dissolved, for two or three times. With good nursings a cure is speedily effected of catarrh or cold, while with carelessness other respiratory organs might be affected and the result prove fatal.

White Scour in Calves.

(*Gastro-Enteritis.*)

This is one of the first diseases to which the calf is subject, and is perhaps less understood by the rearer than any other. Thousands of calves are carried off while of tender age by this disorder; and in too many cases, where it is successfully combated, the animal is so reduced in condition as to take months to reach a state of convalescence. No one dreams of calling in a veterinary surgeon to the young cattle, and even members of the profession would deem such a case *infra dig.;* therefore it is of the greatest importance that each calf-rearer should become fully conversant with the cause of such a common disorder.

Cause.—White scour is brought on from the milk being of inferior quality. The calf is fed with skim milk, or that from an old milch cow deficient in colostrum, or that creamy oily substance called "beastings." This first milk, or beastings, acts as a slight natural purge upon the calf, and clears off any offensive agent from the bowels, and sets them in natural working order. The old milched cow's supply is deficient of this needful quality, hence constipation often sets in. This is followed on by an acid secretion from the lining membrane of the intestines, which coagulates the milk and separates it into component parts. The cheesy part remains as an offensive agent, while the fluid or whey part passes away in the form of white semi-fluid fæces. When an acid secretion is once set up it is a difficult matter to restore a normal state, for every supply of milk acts as a new irritant, even though it be served from a newly-milked cow.

Treatment.—The first effort must be to remove the offending agent, and then restore the natural secretion of the intestinal canal. Port wine, brandy, eggs, and all such potions as are commonly given to stop the looseness are to be strongly condemned, and an oily purge with a sedative may be first given. The following has been advised by a competent veterinary surgeon, and the writer can vouch for its effectiveness :—

Linseed oil	1 pint.
Tincture of opium	1 ounce.
Sweet spirits of nitre	1 ounce.

Give a wine-glass full twice, or even three times, a day, until the bowels begin to act more naturally. The next thing to be done is to restore the natural secretion of the intestines, and the same authority advises as follows :—

Carbonate of potash	1 to 2 drachms.
Powdered rhubarb	1 drachm.
Powdered nutmeg	20 grains.

To be given in a little peppermint water daily. The diet must be in the meantime carefully attended to. Only the best quality of milk must be given from the mother, or a newly-calved cow; and if this is for some reason not obtainable, take half the quantity of milk away, and substitute in its place the same quantity of linseed gruel. This will act as a gentle laxative, and prevent the accumulation of the coagulated milk.

Diarrhœa appears of a different description at times, but more often attacks older animals, and may arise from many complaints, such as catarrh, unwholesome food, &c.; but gastro-enteritis will be defined by attending to our above remarks, and it behoves the breeder to take every precaution to at once arrest a disease which not infrequently leads to death.

Husk or Hoose.

We find this malady prevails more in wet seasons, but few autumns pass into winter without the painful husk being heard in the low-lying pasture fields where young cattle abound. It is seldom found in older beasts than yearlings, although many cases of cough are attributed to this cause that arise from other affections of the lungs.

Cause.—A number of parasitic worms in the windpipe are the cause of this malady. These parasites are from a quarter to half an inch long, and are of a whitish threadlike appearance, and are lodged in a thick viscid mucus, which with the worms almost block up the air-passages of the lungs and irritate the windpipe. So minute are they that they penetrate into the smaller bronchial tubes, and by their continual movement cause constant irritation.

Symptoms.—The attacked calves are found at frequents intervals to be troubled with a distressing hacking cough. The tongue is hung out for some time longer than in the ordinary cough; and another marked feature in the disease is that in a herd many will be attacked at the same time. One symptom follows another in rapid succession, such as emaciation, difficulty in breathing, cessation of rumination, and later on loss of appetitite and diarrhœa. In exceptional instances we have had calves attacked linger on for a month or six weeks, and under liberal feeding gain a mastership over their parasitic foes; but in the majority of cases the owner must be up and doing, or

HUSK OR HOOSE.

in a fortnight or three weeks death will have claimed most of the herd for its own.

The disease has ere now by the ignorant been confounded with pleuro-pneumonia and other affections of the lungs, but a leading symptom in pleuro-pneumonia is a grunt rather than a cough, and moreover only odd cases of this disease are seen at a time, while in husk or hoose nearly every animal in the herd is found attacked. Sometimes the small threadlike worms are coughed up, and in thus endeavouring to dislodge the parasites the poor animal has little rest.

Treatment.—There is only one effectual remedy, and that is to destroy the worms, and then they will soon leave their home. This, however, owing to the sensitive part where they are located, is no easy matter. Oil of turpentine we have found destructive, and is advised by competent authorities to be taken as follows:—

<blockquote>
Linseed oil . . . . 12 ounces.
Oil of turpentine . . . 4 ounces.
</blockquote>

A wine-glass full more or less, according to the size of the calf, to be given twice a day in a little warm gruel.

Inhalation is, however, the surest cure; and Mr. James Law gives advice worthy to be followed. "For the lung parasites, place the affected animals in a close building, and burn pinch after pinch of flowers of sulphur on a piece of paper, laid on an iron shovel, until the air is as much charged with the fumes as they can bear without coughing violently. The administrator must stay with them in the building to avoid accidents, and keep up the application for half an hour at a time. It should be repeated several days in succession, and at intervals of a week for several weeks, so as to kill the young worms as they are hatched out in successive broods; and not until all cough and excitement of breathing have passed should the animal be considered as safe to mix with others or to go on a healthy pasture."

The most liberal feed must be given, to keep up the strength of the animal; and the above-mentioned excellent authority writes—"Feed liberally on linseed cake, rape cake, maize, oats, beans, or other sound nutritious meal diet, to which may be added a mixture in equal parts of sulphate of iron, gentian, and ginger, in proportion of four ounces to every ten calves of three months."

The inhaling method of cure needs to be carried out by a qualified man, or under his careful directions.

Prevention.—Keep the calves off all aftermaths in autumn, and also from all other damp, low-lying land. In September bring them to a shed at night, and do not let them return to pasture in the morning until the grass is perfectly dry, for the worm creeps up the grass when it is moist, and returns to the earth as the moisture leaves the plants. Keep the young cattle in good condition, for then they will be better able to resist the disease.

With regard to aftermath, the author has had several good proofs of the worms prevailing more there; and the likely reason is, that on the grazing land the grass is too short for the worms to get a needful supply of moisture in the hot dry days of summer. We have had a mown field and a grazed one side by side, and a score of calves on the latter escaped, while on the other side the hedge the calves on the aftermath were badly attacked. That good condition tends to keep off the disease we do not doubt; for out of twenty-five calves, one was much more liberally fed, and although lying generally with the other part of the herd it did not suffer, and the remainder had the complaint badly.

The worms, scientifically called *filarcæ bronchiales*, are, as we have before observed, of a thread-like substance, and vary in length. When in a natural state, the lungs of the calf, or some such animal, are their natural home. They are taken in by these animals with moist grass or water, and soon find their way to the windpipe and air-passages of the lungs; and here, if not speedily dislodged, soon breed and multiply, and so prey upon the constitution of the animal as to cause death. To quote again Mr. James Law, the following most interesting information appears upon these worms:—" They are reproduced either in or out of the body. In the first mode the female worm creeps into an air-cell, and there encysts herself and produces eggs or young worms already hatched; or she dies, and the myriad eggs hatching out amid the débris, the young worms finally migrate into the adjacent air-passages, grow to maturity, and reproduce their kind. In the second mode the impregnated female worm is expelled by coughing, and perishes in water, or in moist earth, or on vegetables, and the eggs, escaping from her decomposing remains, may lie unhatched for months, or even a year, or in genial weather may rapidly open and allow the escape of the almost microscopic embryo worms. These in their turn may lie an indefinite period in the water, or moist soil, or on vegetables, and only begin to grow to their mature condition when taken in by a suitable host with food and water. This is true of those of the sheep, goat, and camel, of that of the ox, horse, and ass, and of that of the pig. Only those of the sheep, once introduced into the system, will maintain their place in the lungs for the whole lifetime of the host, though no more young worms should be taken in. That of the ox, &c., on the other hand, is more likely to be expelled, and therefore often infests its host but for a limited period."

Blackleg.

(*Carbuncular Fever.*)

Blackleg is a common disease amongst young stock in certain localities, while in others it is scarcely ever heard of. Again, it sometimes prevails on one farm, and on an adjoining one no case will be known. The writer has had a small field where two cases have occurred in one night, while in the next pasture, divided only by a hedge, no cases have ever fallen out. The disease bears many local names, such as "blackleg," "quarter-ill," "garget," "blood-striking," &c., and it is the most deadly malady to which the bovine species are subject. Indeed, it may be pretty truly said there is no known cure, although one or other questionable practitioners of the empiric type would lead the unwary to suppose the dreaded disease might be pretty easily overcome. Howbeit, we have had many cases amongst our own stock, and many others have come under our eye, yet no life has been saved, although well-qualified veterinary surgeons have been called in. Therefore at present it defeats medical skill, and the disease continues to rage without much chance of being arrested in its progress; and could some reliable remedy be discovered it would be a boon to the breeder, for at present blackleg is a great obstacle to successful rearing.

Symptoms.—It is seldom that the malady is seen in an animal over eighteen months old or under six months, and it more commonly breaks out in the spring-time, when stock is depastured on the fields where the herbage is rich and full of sap. Animals fall when they make a too rapid improvement in their condition, and more often than not the first victims are those that have been much reduced in flesh during winter, and therefore are making the more hasty improvement on the new and luscious pasture. The better bred the animal the more subject it is to attack, simply because it has a greater aptitude to lay on fat. Then the farmer is found to lament losing the best in his herd; while he might know, if more conversant with the disease, that it was owing to the victim's more excellent qualities that it lay doubly open to the disease. The complaint runs at a rapid rate. The animal will be found alone under hedge or tree. A general dulness prevails, and lameness of a severe character is soon noticed. So sudden does the lameness come on that the experienced stockowner concludes the animal is suffering from severe sprain or injury to the part. There is truly an injury to the part, and the lameness is the harbinger of death, which is already hovering over its victim, for the suffering animal is attacked with one of the most fatal blood diseases—the vital fluid is changing in quality, and has a tendency to decompose. Before the attack has extended over many hours a most unmistakable symptom is developed. By placing the hand upon the affected quarter a peculiar crackling is felt under the skin, as if air had been forced in, and wherever this is observable it may be at once known that the ailment is blackleg. It must, however, be distinctly understood, that although the malady may be called blackleg it does not follow that the patient is only attacked in the leg or quarter. The hind leg is certainly the most usual limb to suffer, but it may be the fore leg, neck, back, loin, and, in a very exceptional case, the tongue.

As we have before observed, the disease runs at a rapid rate; in some instances twenty-four or even thirty-six hours will intervene between the commencement of the attack and death, but more often all is over in eighteen hours.

Upon making a *post mortem* examination, when the skin is taken from the affected part, which is usually pretty much puffed up, the tissues are found to be engorged with blood in a gangrenous condition; the internal organs are inflamed and display the same dark-coloured blood; the heart is flabby, and filled with the same dark fluid, partly coagulated; and there is usually effusions of a bloody character in the abdominal cavity.

We scarcely deem it needful to take up space in giving directions for treatment; indeed, if any hopes of successful treatment are to be entertained, the only plan is to call in a veterinary surgeon at the earliest moment, and even then the chance of recovery will be most remote.

Prevention.—In this disease the farmer will be much better repaid for devoting attention to and using means to prevent. First, he should so rear his animals that they never become in low condition, for so sure as poverty is observed in the herd, when the improved condition is made there will be fear of blackleg setting in. If the young animal is found in low condition, the healthy state must be gained very gradually. Second, the fields that have once been found to produce the malady should only be stocked with older cattle, more particularly in the spring time of the year. Get past the middle of June, and in the majority of cases this kind of blood-poisoning will not transpire. Third, in localities where blackleg occurs all young cattle should be pegged, purged, or bled; and if the disease actually breaks out, all these cautions to prevent should be put into force. Pegging is a counter-irritant, and consists in introducing under the skin a piece of black hellebore root, commonly called "bearsfoot," and this sets up a great amount of inflammation. The dewlap under the brisket is the place usually chosen for the seton. Another agent, and one to be more commended, is a seton consisting of equal parts of tow and horsehair, plaited together, and dressed now and then with the following liniment:—

> Venice turpentine . . . . 2 ounces.
> Hog's lard . . . . . . 4 „

This, with gentle heat, should be thoroughly mixed. "Morton's Medicated Cotton" is, on account of needing no dressing, more highly to be commended than either of the other two.

Howbeit, on many farms that the author "kens" full well, calves are reared year by year and no cases of quarter evil arise; and in such instances we counsel stock-raisers not to interrupt nature's laws, which are using him so well, by setoning or otherwise treating his young stock. Land abounding in rich herbage of a slightly costive character is usually more liable to cause this disease, while rather poorer land, that purges a little at times, is generally unproductive of the dire malady.

Ergot in Grasses.

This diseased state of the grasses is not generally understood by farmers; indeed, we have met frequently with many scientific men, educated in plant life, who have been totally ignorant of the existence of such a poison in our grasses. What, then, is ergot? It is a parasitic fungus found in most plants of the grass family, viz., wheat, rye, and almost all the smaller kinds of grass. It is found more largely in rye (*Secale cornutum*) and maize. Balfour observes: "Ergot is a monstrous state of the grain, in which the enlarged and diseased ovary protrudes in a curved form, resembling a cock's spur, hence the name from the French—ergot, meaning a spur. The ovary is black externally, spongy internally, and contains much oily matter. Some consider it as produced by the attack of a fungus, which induces a diseased condition in the ovarian cells. The disease is usually met with in rye, and the name of spurred-rye is ap-

ERGOT IN GRASSES.

plied to it. It sometimes occurs in wheat and in barley; and it has also been noticed in *Lolium perenne* and *Lolium arvense*, *Festuca pretensis*, *Phleum pratense*, *Dactylis glomerata*, *Authoxanthum odoratum*, *Phalaris arundinacea*, and *Alopecurus agrestis*. Ergot consists of a very dense tissue formed by polygonal cells, united ultimately with one another, and filled with an oily fluid. It is developed in the unimpregnated ovule of rye; for although extremely dilated by the eutophyte, and rendered difficult of recognition, the integuments of the ovum increase without completely losing the form which they would have assumed if they had grown into a true grain, imitating in this respect the ovaries of wheat, in which *Tilletia caries* (Bunt) has replaced the seed. The solid mass, which has been called *Sclerotium clavus* by De Candolle, and the filamentous portion, called Sphacelia by Leveillé and Fee, and Ergotætia by Queckett, are only, properly speaking, organs of vegetation. The fungus destined to grow from this apparatus is an elegant Sphæria, probably that called by Fries *Cordyliceps purpurea.*"

Although the above author only seems to have been aware of the parasite existing in such grasses as he has mentioned, we have ourselves found it in many others. The largest specimens have been seen by us in some of the poa grasses, more particularly the Poa aquatica or meadow-sweet grass. (A.) The Cocksfoot (*Dactylis glomerata*) produces fine specimens, as also does (B.) the common rye-grass (*Lolium perenne*). See following illustrations.

A.—A bent of Rye grass (Lolium perenne) showing Ergot spurs.
B.—A head of Cocksfoot grass (Dactylis glomerata) thickly studded with Ergot spurs.

Localities where Found.

Like many of the fungoid family, ergot loves moisture; indeed, it is a *sine quâ non* to its existence in all its stages. Not only damp low-lying soils, but what is far more indispensable, a humid atmosphere. Thus the grasses will be found much more attacked in wet seasons than dry ones, and on such occasions the abortive influences of the spur is more severely felt in our herds and flocks.

Ergot of rye, says Lindley, abounds in many countries, and the Abbé Tessier first visited Sologne to study its effects on the health of the people, and to perform experiments with it on animals. It is grown on wet lands on the Continent amidst the rye crops for medicinal purposes, and in such instances the rye is pulled and sacrificed for the sake of the ergot. The spurs that grow on rye are from one-half to three-quarters of an inch long, while in grasses they vary from only half that size to such minute objects as to be scarcely detectable with the naked eye. As a rule, the finer the kinds of grasses and the more diminutive the flowers and seed, the smaller the ergot is found.

To return to our own pastures. Affected grasses will be observed to abound more on the banks of watercourses, under damp hedges, and on roadsides where overhanging foliage abounds. The author has not succeeded in finding any of the spurs before the latter end of July, nor has the first week in August in any year passed without specimens being discovered. Where the water-grass (*Poa aquatica*) abounds, the spurs will be seen floating on the water in the grasses without much trouble in searching for them.

Its malignant influences are little dreamt of by the majority of graziers. Thousands of cows annually abort upon wet seasons from eating the ergot grain amongst the grass and fodder. It is no imaginary evil, but is an accepted fact amongst those who are competent to speak upon the subject. Howbeit, although the author has over and over again pointed out the facts to different farmers, the words of explanation have been, to a great extent, thrown away.

The action of the ergot, taken in such quantities as it is found in our grasses, acts as an excitant upon the uterus or womb of the pregnant cow, whereby the part contracts, and thus gives the animal a desire to abort the calf. If ergot were taken in large quantities it would have more serious effects, which we will presently show. As before observed, the influence of ergot is not imaginary, for experiments have been made by many men whose veracity cannot be doubted which should convince all who are convincible. It has been given to the mare, the cow, the ewe, the cat, indeed to almost all kinds of pregnant animals, and has never failed to cause untimely birth when given in proper quantities and when the animal had become advanced to a certain stage in pregnancy.

In many instances a cow aborts in a herd, and quickly many more follow suit. This is commonly attributed to some infection or sympathy caused by the other animals smelling of the aborted remains of the foetus. This, as the Scotch say, has not been proven; but it is proved beyond a doubt that ergot

ERGOT IN GRASSES.

will cause these mishaps. Again, allowing for a moment the sympathetic theory, how, pray, comes the first cow to abort? It is quite clear that many cases assigned to sympathy are really caused by the poisonous ergot; and having visited many pastures besides our own, where complaints of the misdoing of the cows had been heard, we found in most instances the grasses were thickly beset with the spur, while no other reasonable cause could account for the losses.

Having now shown the evil influences that this parasitic fungus causes among home herds of cattle, it will be well to give some reliable historic records which will show how potent is the fungus. We should here state that ergot of rye or maize and such as are found on our common grasses are each of the same nature, and are as useful in medicine as disastrous in careless use or when taken inadvertently in food. To again quote from Lindley : " Ergot of maize is, according to Roulin, very common in Columbia, and the use of it is attended with a shedding of the hair, and even the teeth, of both man and beast. Mules fed on it lose their hoofs, and fowls lay eggs without shells. Its action on the uterus is often as powerful as that of rye ergot, or perhaps more so. The country name of the maize thus affected is 'maïspeladero.'"

The condition induced when an animal partakes of ergot for some time is termed ergotism. One large dose induces in man and animals dryness and irritation of the throat, salivation, thirst, burning pain in the stomach, vomiting, colic, and sometimes diarrhœa. Cerebral symptoms, such as headache, giddiness, and stupor, are also met with (Taylor). The chronic effects have been observed by Tessier on birds and pigs; by M. Bonjean on birds and dogs; by Parola on solipedes; and by Descote on ruminants. The first effect is to produce loss of appetite and stupefaction; when it begins to act, dogs howl frightfully until they are completely under its influence, and then lie down and groan. The most usual symptoms are dull, stupid expression; staring look, dilated pupils, vertigo, signs of inebriation, coma; tremors, convulsive twitchings, tetanic spasms, especially of hind limbs, and the latter soon become feeble and paralysed; the animal can scarcely stand upright, moves slowly and with difficulty; there is general debility and loss of flesh; pulse slow and weak; skin cold; coat staring. The extremities, ears, horns, and tail, have lost their natural temperature; there is a sero-mucous or sometimes bloody discharge from the nose; the limbs are œdematous; black spots, livid patches, and gangrenous sores form on the surface of the body; dry gangrene of beak and tongue of birds, of the ears, tail, and the phalanges of the limbs, and these parts separate slowly and without pain from the living tissue adjoining.

"When in Lyons I saw a case of ergotism in man. Both hands were black and dead, with a distinct mark of separation above the wrist. They were amputated by M. Valette."

Most frightful disasters have occurred in bygone years when rye bread was more largely eaten, from the mixture of ergot with the flour. At the beginning of the last century this diseased condition of the rye occurred in France to such an extent that in consequence there were no fewer than 500 patients at one time under the care of the surgeons at the public hospital at Orleans. The symptoms first came on with the appearance of drunkenness, after which the toes became diseased, mortified, and fell off. The disorder then extended itself up the leg, and frequently attacked the trunk, and this sometimes occurred even after amputation of the diseased limbs had been performed, in the vain hope of stopping the progress of the disorder. Notwithstanding all its baneful influences elsewhere, ergot is much used in medicines by both the human surgeon and the veterinary practitioners, chiefly to hasten on cases of prolonged labour, and for such cases ergot of rye is generally procured—being more easily obtained. If, however, our grass ergot were used, it might be a means of helping to exterminate the parasite.

Its different States.

In late autumn the ergot grain falls to the ground, when fully matured, with the grass seeds, and in this situation it remains throughout the winter, but slightly protected from the inclemency of the weather, until early summer, and then a most peculiar change takes place, and one that for a long time puzzled clever botanists. Instead of the grain or spur bursting into life like other grains, it shows that it belongs to the fungoid order of plants. Several minute mushroom-shaped objects grow from the grain, the stem of which is of a purple colour, about an inch long, and nearly transparent. Upon the stem is a small head, similar to that of a pin. These are called the true fungi (*Claviceps purpurea*). Seen under a microscope, the heads contain many chambers, and in a few days the fungus ripens and throws off innumerable invisible spores. Such as happen to settle upon any of the grasses when in bloom ingraft themselves into the seed-case, as it were, and raise the natural germ or seed from its position. Having taken possession of the situation, they commence at once to grow as parasites, nourished by the plants as foster-parents. The spores begin floating in the air about the time most of the grasses come into bloom, at the beginning of June, and from that time until autumn the spores are growing into the perfect spur.

Howbeit, there is yet another stage in the life of ergot—when seeds are produced capable of propagating the disease. When the ergot is nearly or quite full grown, there will be observed at the end of the spur an apex or growth. This apex develops spores which fungoligists term *spermatico* or *conidia*, of the early or *sphacelia* state of the parasite. These spores are released by the grasses being blown together, or more often from being swilled down by rain. Thus we have noticed a spur or two on the tops of plants, and in a few weeks many of the seed chambers below are also taken possession of by the parasite. Therefore heads of grass will seldom be found with only one spur in if attacked at all, *i.e.*, supposing the second spores (*spermatia*) of the *sphacelia* state have had time to develop. The apex of the ergot under powerful microscopic observation is a wonderful sight indeed.

When the ergot arrives at the mature state the most danger is to be apprehended. Later on, towards the close of the year, the spur falls to the ground, and thus the same routine is annually continued and a dangerous parasite flourishes, little hindered or troubled about by the stock-keeper to whom such heavy losses are caused. We have ourselves several times produced the *Claviceps purpurea* by plucking some spurs and burying them in the earth until spring and then giving plenty of moisture.

Means of Eradication.

Bearing in mind that plants are only attacked when in full bloom, and that after the spores rest upon the flower-cells the spur is at least a month before it reaches its mature state, it should be the object to cut all meadow grasses before the latter condition of the ergot is reached. Nothing is otherwise lost in the value of the hay. It is far better cut at such a period before the grass seeds ripen, and it may be taken as an accepted fact that if the grass seeds have not ripened, neither has the ergot spur matured, therefore reproduction is prevented. Howbeit, when the mowing fields have been cleared many water-grasses that grow upon the banks of rivers, their tributaries, ditches, ponds, and also hedges, contain the fungus, and such grasses should be cut down to prevent the pest being propagated.

Another method that has been suggested is handpicking, but this in most cases must be discarded on account of the heavy expense. Still, ergot might to a certain extent be picked from the coarser grasses, or rather the grasses be plucked that contain it, and it is to the coarser grasses that it more freely adheres. Again, if it could be sold to chemists for medical purposes in place of the ergot of rye, which is chiefly obtained from abroad, it would then partly or altogether repay for gathering, and the peasantry would reap benefit from the labour, and our plants become considerably freed from this parasite.

In old pasture-fields we can only further advise the grass to be grazed down pretty bare in such damp localities where ergot is likely to prevail. It will ever be found that this fungus flourishes better and is more dependent upon a humid atmosphere than upon moisture actually in the soil. Nevertheless, land should be drained, for doubtless a greater amount of moisture rises from wet, ill-drained land, than from such as lies high and dry. Our readers will only find the grasses more thickly beset with the spores on the higher lands when the season is a rainy one, like several we have lately experienced; seasons that produce the dreaded fluke insect that plays such mischief with our flocks are also productive of such fungoid diseases in our grasses as mildew and ergot.

Old coarse grasses grow up and die down from year to year in the rich feeding pastures, too sour for cattle to eat, and these are, more than all others, suitable nurse-plants for this parasitic fungus. If these grasses were cut in the early part of July the ergot would be destroyed, and the herbage would make some good hay, while the pasture would be left sweet, so that animals would feed upon it. Further, a dressing of salt should be applied, which ever tends to promote the growth of fine grasses and the destruction of coarse ones. Moreover, cattle and sheep feed freely where salt has been applied, and thus the plants are prevented from running to seed.

In conclusion, we call the attention of landlords, tenants, and scientific men to the importance of this subject, as being worthy of their most serious attention, for losses one year with another from abortion and other animal ailments incurred by ergot in Britain may be estimated at as much as is caused by foot-and-mouth disease. The subject is of vital importance to landlords and tenants, because of the heavy losses sustained, while to the man of science the study is full of interest. Up till the present time the whole matter has been overlooked; and should the remarks we have made in this manual lead but in a small degree to the destruction of this deadly parasite, the attention bestowed upon the subject will not have been in vain. At least, we trust to have agitated a theme that will engage the intelligent study of those most interested; hence we shall have gained a step towards the total extermination of a most poisonous parasite from our pastures.

INDEX.

	PAGE
ABORTION—causes	92
Unwholesome food	93
Unwholesome water	93
Ill-treatment	94
Sympathy	94
Fright	95
Age—definition of	40
Of a cow	41
Tampering with horns	41
Professor Simonds on teeth	43
Tabulated register of	44-45
Alderney—	15
Points of merit	16
Advancement of the breed	17
Ayrshire—description of	5
Milking qualities of	6
BLACK-LEG (carbuncular fever)	110-114
Breeder's cow	18
Age to buy in	19
Best kinds	20
Bag or udder	21-24
Milk veins	24
Buttercups—wholesome	37
Cows—	
Mixed breeds advised	29
Constitution, the	32
A good milker	33, 34

	PAGE
Cows—different breeds of	4
Aldorney	15
Ayrshire	5
Breeder's cow	18
Cottier's cow	35
Dairyman's cow	28
English breed of cows	7
Gentleman's cow	14
Hereford	10
Kerry	39
London cow	30
Where grazed	31
Longhorns	12
Milkseller's cow	28
Pembroke	38
Scotch breeds	5
Shorthorns	7
Suffolk Dun	13
Calf—treatment of	85
Purchased foods for	86
Treatment at birth	87
From one to three months	89
From three to six months	89, 90
Best kinds for rearing	91
Catarrh or cold	102
Cottier's cow, the	35
Unhealthy or limited space	36
Creamer, the	78
Illustration	79
Its advantages	80-83
The water-supply	83

INDEX.

	PAGE
DAIRY, the	75
Churning	76
Construction of dairy	77
Creamer advised	78
Diseases of animals	92
Disposing of the cow	71
ENGLISH breed of cows	7
Engorgement of the rumen	101
Ergot in grasses	114
Illustrations	116
Localities where found	117
Its malignant influences	118
Historic records	119
Its different state	121
Means of eradication	123-125
FOOD for dairy cows	61-64
Method of feeding	65
Foot and mouth disease (*Eczema epizootica*)	96-98
GENTLEMAN'S cow, the	14
Gestation, treatment during	52-57
HEREFORD, the—its qualities	10
Colour, &c.	11
Hoven or blown (*Tympanitis*)	99-101
Husk or hoose	106-108
Worms, the	109
INTRODUCTION — Wheat-growing will not pay	1-3

	PAGE
KERRY cow, the	39
Much in demand	39
Its qualities	40
LONGHORNS	12
Their former homes	13
MILKSELLER'S cow, the	28
Milk—its value	35
Mammary glands, the	40
Manurial value of food	66
Milking—kindness needed	67
Care in drying	69
Qualities of milk	69
PARTURITION — treatment during	57-61
Pembroke cow, the	38
Purchasing the cow	46
Symmetry preferred to size	47
To avoid "screws"	48
Judgment needed in purchasing	49, 50
Preferable to buy at home	51
SALT—its value	74
Shorthorn, the	7
Its qualities	8
Points of merit	9
Stall fatting	72-74
Suffolk Dun, the	13
TOUCH, the	25, 26
WHITE SCOUR, the (*Gastroenteritis*)	103-105

PRINTED BY BALLANTYNE, HANSON AND CO.
EDINBURGH AND LONDON.

ADVERTISEMENTS.

DAIRY SUPPLY COMPANY,
LIMITED.

TRADE  MARK.

28 and 29 Museum Street,
35, 36, and 37 Little Russell Street, and
Duke Street Factory,
} LONDON, W.C.
(all adjoining).

Manufacturers of every Description of
Dairy Utensils for Butter, Cheese, Farm, Town, or Private Dairies.

AGENTS FOR ALL DAIRY PATENTS.

SOLE AGENTS FOR THE
DE LAVAL CREAM SEPARATOR, THE VERTICAL DRUM SEPARATOR, THE DELAITEUSE, TULLEY'S EGG BOXES for Road or Rail.

Patentees of the Lady's Churn, Barham's Percentage Lactometer, for instantly detecting Water in Milk.

MILKING PAILS, CHINA DAIRY WARE,
&c. &c., sent to the Colonies, and all parts of the World.

The same attention paid to Small Orders as Large ones.

Illustrated Catalogue free.

IMPORTANT TO CALF-REARERS.

TWELVE REASONS WHY

HENRI'S PATENT CALF-REARING FEED

SHOULD BE USED BY ALL CALF-REARERS.

1st.—Because there is no trouble to get the Calves to eat it.
2nd.—Because Calves like it better than milk, and take to it eagerly.
3rd.—Because it PREVENTS SCOUR, and gives Calves a good healthy coat.
4th.—Because Calves thrive, grow fast, and do well upon it.
5th.—Because it is an UNEQUALLED SUBSTITUTE FOR MILK.
6th.—Because it is the best, cheapest, and most nutritious food for Calves.
7th.—Because Calves will not "fall off" when "turned out" to dry food.
8th.—Because Calves can be reared upon it from 14 days old.
9th.—Because double the number of Calves can be reared on the same quantity of milk.
10th.—Because Calves reared on it are bigger at 12 months old than if reared with any other article.
11th.—Because yearling Calves can be sold for more money than when reared exclusively on milk.
12th.—Because it never varies in quality, and is, without egotism, the best in the market.

Testimonials as to the Value of

HENRI'S PATENT CALF-REARING FEED.

EXCELLENT MILK SUBSTITUTE!
LEICESTER.—Mr. JNO. W. WARD, Burton Overy, says:—"Having used several different kinds of Cattle Feed, I find *none so good as Henri's*. For rearing calves, I find the Calf-Rearing Feed an *excellent substitute for milk*, and *they do well* after it."

NOT A SINGLE CASE OF SCOUR!
LOUTH.—Mr. THOS. MARSHALL, Ludborough, says:—"I have used your Calf-Rearing Feed for two years, and can truly say *it is very valuable*. I had *not a single case of scour*, and used very little milk indeed."

THE BEST EVER TRIED!
DERBY.—Mrs. W. ORME, Heath House, Foston, says:—"I have used your Calf Feed the last three years, and have great pleasure in recommending it to any one wishing for *a substitute for milk*. The Calves are fond of it, and *free from scour*. It is the best preparation I have ever tried."

BEST FOR CALVES!
LEEK.—Mr. W. L. WAINE, Hanfield Farm, Cheddleton, says:—"I think your Calf-Rearing Feed is *the best I have used* for Calves, and for *preventing scour*, and is *a saving of milk*."

BEATS ALL OTHER "FOODS!"
GRANTHAM.—Mr. WM. LUPTON, Hanby, says:—"I used your Calf-Rearing Feed last winter with *great success*, and can *strongly recommend* it, as my *Calves did better on it than on anything else I have had*."

Price 4s. per cwt. Bag; 21s. per ½ cwt. Bag. Carriage paid to any Railway Station or Wharf.

For Directions for Use, Testimonials, and other particulars of

HENRI'S PATENT CALF-REARING FEED,

write for Pamphlet, which will be sent post-free on application to

HENRI'S PATENT CATTLE FEED COMPANY,

(Manufacturers of Henri's Patent Horse Condition Powders,)
STEAM MILLS REFORM ST., HULL.

ADVERTISEMENTS.

THORLEY'S FOOD FOR CATTLE
WILL BE FOUND OF
GREAT VALUE FOR STALL FEEDING.

By its use all animals are kept in perfect health, it causes them to eat their food with a relish and fatten quickly. THORLEY'S FOOD will convert straw into a superior Provender; if mixed at time of chaff-cutting it imparts a pleasant flavour, renders it more digestible, Stock eat it greedily, and prevents all waste. Sold in Cases and Bags.

The Principal Prize-Winners at all Fat-Stock Shows fed on Thorley's.

LACTIFER, A MEAL FOR CALVES.
Is the most reliable substitute for Milk in the Market. Prevents Scour.

Thousands of unsolicited testimonials. Avoid the numerous imitations in the market. Buy only from the well-known Establishment. THORLEY'S have been before the public nearly forty years, and still stand unrivalled.

JOSEPH THORLEY, King's Cross, London,
Cattle Food Manufacturer by Royal Warrant to H.M. the Queen.

TAYLOR'S VETERINARY MEDICINES.

TAYLOR'S BLACK MIXTURE, unequalled for colic or gripes in Horse, and Calves purging, &c. Bottles, 1s. 6d. each.
TAYLOR'S GENERAL COW DRINK, unequalled for stoppage or maw-bound, milk fever, blain, longslough, or garget, drying yellows, blown, &c. 1s. each; 11s. per dozen.
TAYLOR'S CLEANSING DRINK for new-calved cows, to remove the cleansing. 9d. each; 8s. per dozen.
TAYLOR'S HOOSE MIXTURE for Calves. 4s. per quart bottle.
TAYLOR'S DRESSING FOR FOOT ROT. Bottles, 1s. and 2s.
TAYLOR'S RED OILS, for stake wounds in horses, lameness, injuries, &c. Half-pints, 1s.; pints, 2s.; quarts, 3s. 6d.
TAYLOR'S TONIC AND ALTERATIVE POWDERS, in 1 lb. tins, 1s.; 14 lb. boxes, 12s. 6d.
TAYLOR'S COUGH POWDERS OR BALLS. 2s. 6d. per packet.

TAYLOR'S "DERBY" CALF MEAL.
In Bags—1 cwt., 21s.; ½ cwt., 11s. 6d. (Less five per cent. prompt cash.) Carriage paid to nearest station. Unequalled.

PREPARED ONLY BY
THOMAS TAYLOR, M.R.C.V.S.L.,
AT THE STEAM MILLS, VICTORIA STREET, DERBY.
To be had of most Corn Dealers, Chemists, &c.

N.B.—Any of the above Veterinary Medicines sent by parcel post on receipt of stamps.

T. TAYLOR, M.R.C.V.S., proprietor of the Veterinary Medicines and Derby Calf Meal advertised in all the Agricultural papers, having had the medical care of the horses belonging to the Midland Railway, Bass & Co., and Allsopp & Co. for more than thirty years, will be glad to give advice to any gentlemen on diseases of their stock Gratis. A caution is held out against the nostrums advertised by chemists and unqualified persons, who can know nothing of the treatment of disease, and which must end in disappointment. A case of assorted medicines sent carriage paid on receipt of postal order for 21s.

THE LANCASTER CALF FOOD
MANUFACTURED BY
CARRUTHERS & CO., LANCASTER.
ESTABLISHED 1788.

Manufacturers of Special Meals for Cattle for over 25 Years. Price 12s. per cwt. at their Mills or Lancaster Stations (Cash with Order).

From THOS. W. KEY, Old Hall, Casterton, Kirkby Lonsdale, Westmorland.

In answer to your inquiries as to the merits of your Calf Meal, I am glad to say that having now used it for several years, I can bear full testimony that it is the best food I have ever used for Calves, as it keeps them free from scour, in a healthy thriving condition, and full of hair. I have recommended it to several of my neighbours, and trust they will give it a trial if they have not yet done so. I shall continue to use it.

From THOMAS KITCHEN, Tatham Old Hall, Wennington near Lancaster.

During the last few years I have reared over 100 Calves with your "Calf Food," without a single case of "Hyan" or "Blackleg," and free from "Scour" or "Hoose." I believe the "Calf Food" while used is a certain preventative of the above ailments, and is certainly the best treatment I know of for rearing Calves in sound, healthy, vigorous condition.

From THOS. DOBSON, Brotherton, Ferry Bridge, Yorkshire.

Will you please forward another bag of your Calf Food to Ferry Bridge Station, P.O.O. for 12s. enclosed. Your Calf Food has done well for our calves, and I have a yearling foal which was very near eaten up with worms, I gave it some Calf Food which has entirely removed the worms, and the foal is now doing well.

From W. LAWRENSON, Johnson's Farm, Out Rawcliffe, Garstang, Lancashire.

I have used your Calf Food for a considerable time past. It has done exceedingly well for my calves. I gave it to a yearling colt which it improved immensely, and I sold it a few months afterwards to Mr Bashall's steward for £100.

From ABBOTT & WINSTER, Shap, Westmorland.

Having used the "Lancaster Calf Food" for several years, and many of our neighbours having done the same, we can give it the highest recommendation for rearing calves in sound, healthy, and hardy condition, free from scour and worms, and much less liable to hoose, than under any other treatment we know of. We have proved the Calf Food to be equally good for general stock, We have this winter fed three heifers, giving them two parts of Calf Food to one part of oatmeal; all sold for high prices, and killed a first-class quality of beef, one of them having taken five prizes at the Lancaster, Penrith (beating twelve grand heifers), Manchester, and Stalybridge Fat Shows, and was declared by experienced butchers and stock owners wherever she was exhibited to be the nearest to perfection they had ever seen in stock feeding. We believe that all they who advertise in agricultural journals that their horses, foals, cows, calves, pigs, or other stock, are suffering from hoose, husk, worms, or from any other cause are not thriving satisfactorily, would find an immediate benefit by using the "Lancaster Calf Food."

Please forward Directed Envelope to " Carruthers & Co., Lancaster," for full particulars and Testimonials from a large number of most experienced Farmers.

ADVERTISEMENTS.

The Cheapest and Best Food for
PIGS, CATTLE, & POULTRY.

Superior to Indian or Barley Meal
IN FOOD VALUE.

CHEAPER IN PRICE.

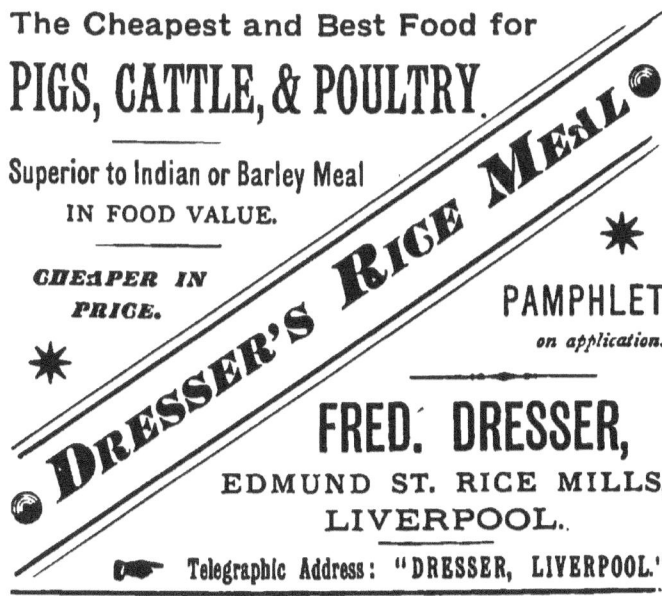

DRESSER'S RICE MEAL

PAMPHLET
on application.

FRED. DRESSER,
EDMUND ST. RICE MILLS,
LIVERPOOL.

☞ Telegraphic Address: "DRESSER, LIVERPOOL."

BENNETT'S BERKELEY VALE
CALF MEAL.
THE CHEAPEST AND BEST MILK SUBSTITUTE IN THE MARKET.
REQUIRES NO BOILING.　　PREVENTS SCOUR.

PRICE 21s. PER CWT. CARRIAGE PAID.

Read the following testimony of those who use it:—
From Mr PETER, *Steward to Lord Fitzhardinge.*

HAM, BERKELEY, *Sept. 12th, 1885.*

DEAR SIR,—I should feel obliged if you would kindly send on the 5 cwt. Calf Meal I ordered of you the other day. I am highly pleased with it. I find it a capital substitute for milk, a preventative of scour, and it keeps the animal healthy and growing at a much less cost than milk.—Yours truly, 　　JAMES PETER.

BROOKLANDS, FALFIELD, *Oct. 6th, 1885.*

DEAR SIR,—Send me on another lot of Bennett's Calf Meal; the 6 cwt. I had of you is all gone—I cannot speak too highly of it. It is a good preventative of scour, and a very economical means of rearing Calves.—Yours truly, 　　G. STRICKLAND.
Mr T. IND, *Yate.*

MANUFACTURED BY
JOHN BENNETT, Cam, Dursley, Gloucestershire.
AGENTS WANTED IN UNREPRESENTED DISTRICTS.

8th Season 1886.

CORPORATION OF THE CITY OF MANCHESTER

THE MANCHESTER CORPORATION CON-CENTRATED MANURE made from Urine, Excrement, Blood, Bones, and Offal, from the City Abattoirs, and Fish, &c., from the Markets, containing about

3 per cent. Ammonia,
7 per cent. Phosphates,
30 per cent. Organic Matter, with Potash, Salts, &c.

Analysis Guaranteed.

PRICE, £3 PER TON.

The Manure is in nice condition, having the appearance and touch of fine mould. It contains all the constituents necessary to render the soil fertile. The Ammonia is in a form which promotes growth, and the amount of it (3 per cent.) is an important feature.

The removal from the City of the material from which the Manure is made *being an absolute necessity*, Profit has not been considered in fixing the price.

It is packed in Bags, each containing 1 cwt., which are not returnable, and will be delivered at any Railway Station within 50 miles of Manchester in quantities of not less than 2 Tons, beyond 50 and within 150 miles in lots of not less than 4 Tons, at £3 per Ton, with the following discount, viz. :—5 per cent. for cash within one month, 2½ per cent. within three months, net cash after three months. Special terms for distances exceeding 150 miles.

Orders booked in rotation, and, as supply is limited, no guarantee given as to actual date of delivery of Manure ordered late in season.

For Samples and further particulars apply to H. WHILEY, Superintendent, Town Hall, Manchester.

ADVERTISEMENTS.

BAMBER & CO.'S
CELEBRATED CHURNS

Are recommended by ALL who use them.

They are EASE, SIMPLICITY, and UTILITY combined.

ILLUSTRATED CATALOGUE POST FREE.

DAIRY IMPLEMENT WORKS,
PRESTON, LANCASHIRE.

ADVERTISEMENTS.

THE "COOLEY" PATENT PORTABLE CREAMER.

The American Deep Setting Submerged System of Raising Cream in 12 Hours, or between Milkings.

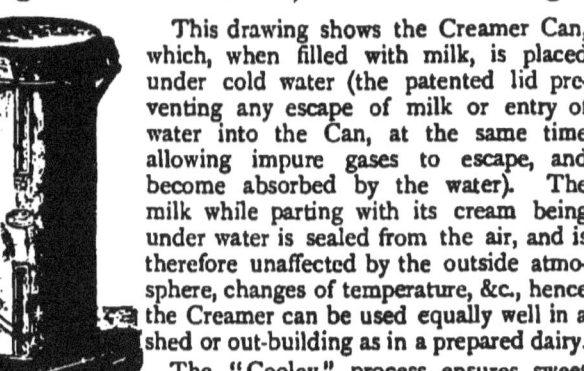

This drawing shows the Creamer Can, which, when filled with milk, is placed under cold water (the patented lid preventing any escape of milk or entry of water into the Can, at the same time allowing impure gases to escape, and become absorbed by the water). The milk while parting with its cream being under water is sealed from the air, and is therefore unaffected by the outside atmosphere, changes of temperature, &c., hence the Creamer can be used equally well in a shed or out-building as in a prepared dairy.

The "Cooley" process ensures sweet cream and milk winter and summer. It yields more cream than any other system, saves labour in manipulation, and is the most rapid and economical process of extracting cream from milk.

Prospectus and Testimonials post-free from the Patentees,

LLOYD, LAWRENCE, & CO.,
34 WORSHIP STREET, LONDON, E.C.

ADVERTISEMENTS.

R. A. LISTER & CO.'S
New Double Roller "BEAUFORT HUNT" CORN CRUSHER,
BROUGHT OUT IN 1885.

See Notice in *The Field*, 24th October 1885.

Price, as above illustrated 52/6
Price, for Man and Boy, with shaft projecting at both sides and two handles . . 57/6
Sent on a MONTH'S TRIAL, Carriage paid, to any Railway Station.
May be had from any good Ironmonger, or direct from

R. A. LISTER & CO., Dursley, Gloucestershire,

Makers of Chaff Cutters, Cake Breakers, Farmers' Stone Grinding Mills, &c.

TO FARMERS, GRAZIERS, AND OTHERS.

'THE MAGNET'

Agricultural & Commercial Gazette.

PRICE THREEPENCE HALFPENNY.

'THE MAGNET,' the Largest and Best of all the Agricultural Newspapers, is published every Monday Afternoon in time for Post, and contains :—

Full and Latest Reports of the London Corn and Cattle Markets;

The Seed Market; Hop Market;

The Wool Trade; Provincial Markets and Fairs;

TOGETHER WITH

Original Reviews of the Corn Trade; Essays on Practical Farming; Contributions by Experienced Writers on British and Foreign Agriculture;

And a Variety of Miscellaneous Information important to Farmers, Cattle-Breeders, Graziers, and others.

It is also an excellent FAMILY NEWSPAPER, containing all the General News of the Week, FOREIGN and DOMESTIC, circulating largely in the Agricultural Districts.

SPORTING NOTES AND PREDICTIONS by "PEGASUS."

'The Magnet' is a First-Class Medium for Advertisements.

Offices: 19 EXETER STREET, STRAND.

The ✠ Farmer
AND
CHAMBER OF AGRICULTURE
JOURNAL.

(FORTY-SECOND YEAR.)

This Journal is now published as a PENNY NEWSPAPER, and gives all the Agricultural News of the Week, the Latest Markets, together with numerous Original Articles by the Leading Writers of the day on the Corn Trade, the Breeding, Grazing, and Dairy Interests, Poultry, &c. The FARMER may be ordered through any Newsagent, at the Railway Bookstalls, or it will be supplied direct from the Office, 291 Strand, W.C.

EVERY MONDAY, ONE PENNY.

Subscription, post-free, - - - 6s. 6d. per annum.
,,   ,,   - - - 3s. 6d. for Six Months.
,,   ,,   - - - 1s. 9d. for Three Months.
REMITTANCES PAYABLE TO JOHN HALL.

Specimen Copies, One Month, post-free for Sixpence.

ADVERTISEMENTS.

THE
AGRICULTURAL GAZETTE,
DAIRY FARMER.

MONDAY.   [*Established 1844.*]   **TWOPENCE.**

The AGRICULTURAL GAZETTE has for many years, by consent of all, stood at the head of the English Agricultural Press. It is unequalled as a high-class farmer's paper, and is now sold at TWOPENCE weekly, or post-free, 10s. 10d. for a whole year.

It is read very extensively in all parts of England, as well as in foreign countries; and the following extracts from letters, &c., indicate how highly it is valued by its Subscribers:—

1. "A wonderful twopenny worth."—F. W.
2. "The best value I have ever seen."—G. T.
3. "The best example of a good agricultural paper we have ever seen."—*Morning Post.*
4. "I attribute whatever success I have had to reading the *A. G.*"—H. T.
5. "The most useful paper I have ever read. Every farmer would do well to become a subscriber."—T. B., jun.
6. "I will take it as long as I live. It is the best paper published."—J. S. B.
7. "I can honestly say it is worth to me, on account of the valuable information I get from it, as many pounds a year as its cost in pence.—W. J. E.

UNEQUALLED AS AN ADVERTISING MEDIUM
Amongst the well-to-do Agricultural and Provincial Classes.

Advertisers are particularly desired to note that the Proprietors of the AGRICULTURAL GAZETTE state the actual *bona fide* circulation of the paper, and that to every Advertiser is given the following

CERTIFICATE AND GUARANTEE OF CIRCULATION.
"*It is hereby certified and guaranteed that the regular ordinary circulation of the* Agricultural Gazette *numbers 5400 to 6000 copies weekly, and it is further hereby provided that the holder hereof, or authorised representative, may test the accuracy of this Certificate by at any time inspecting the Publisher's Books for any number of weeks desired.*

"JAMES MACDONALD, *Managing Director.*"

ADVERTISING RATES MODERATE.
LIBERAL REDUCTION FOR LONG SERIES.

Terms of Subscription.
Post-free—3 Months, 2s. 9d.; 6 Months, 5s. 6d.; 12 Months, 10s. 10d.

VINTON & CO., LIMITED,
9 NEW BRIDGE STREET, LUDGATE CIRCUS, LONDON, E.C.

ADVERTISEMENTS.

One Penny Weekly. Monthly, 6d.

AGRICULTURE,
The only Illustrated Agricultural Journal Published at One Penny.

Published every MONDAY EVENING in time for mails.

SUBSCRIPTION IN ADVANCE.
6s. 6d. per Annum, Post-Free; 3s. 3d. Six Months, Post-Free; 1s. 8d. Three Months, Post-Free.

P.O.O. should be made payable to C. EGLINGTON, *Money Order Department, General Post Office, London.*

AGRICULTURE has already a larger and more influential circulation than any of the old-established Journals.

ADVERTISEMENTS—SCALE OF CHARGES.
CHARGE FOR SINGLE INSERTIONS.—Twenty-five words or less in body type, 2s.; each additional line of about nine words, 6d. Across two columns, per inch 12s.; across three columns, per inch 18s.; whole page, £10.

CHARGE FOR SERIAL ADVERTISEMENTS.
SINGLE COLUMN.—6 insertions at 5s. 6d. per inch per insertion.
    13 ,,   5s. 0d. ,,   ,,
    26 or more   4s. 0d. ,,   ,,
ACROSS TWO COLUMNS.—6 insertions at 11s. 0d. per inch per insertion.
    13 ,,   10s. 0d. ,,   ,,
    26 or more   8s. 0d. ,,   ,,
ACROSS THREE COLUMNS.—6 insertions at 16s. 6d. ,,   ,,
    13 ,,   15s. 0d. ,,   ,,
    26 or more   12s. 0d. ,,   ,,

No trade advertisement inserted at a less price than 2s. *net* per insertion.

BAILIFFS AND OTHERS WANTING SITUATIONS.—25 words or less, 2s. Paragraphs per line, 1s.

Advertisements for ensuing number should reach the office on Saturday morning to ensure insertion. No advertisement can be "altered" or "stopped" after Monday morning's post. Advertisers not having a regular account are requested to accompany their advertisements by a remittance. All letters to be addressed to the PUBLISHER, 26 Catherine Street, Strand, W.C.

AGRICULTURE can be obtained from any of Messrs W. H. SMITH & SON'S Bookstalls, of all the Wholesale News Agents in the United Kingdom, or direct from the

PUBLISHING OFFICES, 26 Catherine Street, Strand, LONDON, W.C.

'LAND & WATER'

(ESTABLISHED 1866,)

A Sporting, Farming, and Country Gentleman's Newspaper.

REDUCED TO 3d. WEEKLY.

A FIRST-CLASS JOURNAL
FOR
SPORTSMEN, AGRICULTURISTS, AND COUNTRY GENTLEMEN,

Each issue containing Special Reports—with Comments and Articles—of the Week's doing in

Hunting, Turf, Shooting and Kennel, Coursing, Coaching, Fishing, Yachting, Rowing, Swimming, Running, Athletics (with Special Reports from the Public Schools), Cricket, Chess, Agriculture, Horticulture, Estate Management, and Practical Natural History.

SPECIMEN COPY sent free of charge on application, and mentioning this Work.

SUBSCRIPTION:
United Kingdom, 15s. per annum; Foreign, 17s. 6d. per annum; including Postage.

Publishing Offices: 182 STRAND, LONDON, W.C.

ADVERTISEMENTS.

THE
Estates Gazette

AND

INVESTMENT RECORD

(ESTABLISHED 1858).

A JOURNAL DEVOTED TO LAND AND HOUSE PROPERTY.

Contains Articles and Notes relating to Land and the Land Market.

An Important Feature of the Paper is the

Accurate List of Forthcoming Sales, and the Results of such Sales,

Published with the sanction of the Committee of the Estate Exchange

RESIDENCES AND FARMS TO BE LET OR SOLD.

Single Copy, Price 3d.   Annual Subscription, 16s. (prepaid).

OFFICE FOR ADVERTISEMENTS—

6 FETTER LANE, FLEET STREET,
LONDON.

POULTRY AILMENTS
AND THEIR TREATMENT.

An Invaluable Handbook for Poultry-Keepers, containing Plain Instructions for the Treatment of all Poultry Diseases.

By D. J. THOMSON GRAY (Psyche),
Editor, "Scottish Fancier and Rural Gazette."

Post-free, 1s. 1d.   Cloth Covers, 1s. 8d.

JAMES P. MATHEW & CO., 17 and 19 Cowgate, Dundee.

MAD DOGS AND HYDROPHOBIA
By HUGH DALZIEL,
*Author of " British Dogs," " Diseases of Dogs," " Training of Dogs,"
" Diseases of Horses," &c.
Kennel Editor of " The Bazaar and Country."
And formerly Kennel Editor of " The Stock-Keeper;" and Kennel Reporter
and Critic of " The Field," &c.*

POST-FREE - - 1s. 1d.

JAMES P. MATHEW & CO., 17 and 19 Cowgate, Dundee.

The Scottish Fancier & Rural Gazette
A MONTHLY ILLUSTRATED JOURNAL.

DEVOTED TO THE BREEDING, MANAGEMENT, AND EXHIBITION OF

Dogs, Poultry, Pigeons, Cage Birds, Rabbits,
AND OTHER PET STOCK.

It is the only Paper of the kind published in Scotland, and the first authority on the subjects it professes to treat of. Exists entirely for the fanciers, whose friend it is. Is pointed and fearless in its criticism, and full of practical information for the Breeder, Exhibitor, and Amateur.

Price 2d. ; Post-free, 2½d.

SUBSCRIPTION—2s. 6d. per Annum.

JAMES P. MATHEW & CO., 17 and 19 Cowgate, Dundee.

'FISHING,'
AN ILLUSTRATED JOURNAL
FOR THE
ANGLER, FLY FISHER, FISH CULTURIST, AND NATURALIST.

Every Friday Evening, One Penny.

"FISHING" consists of 16 pages folio, and illustrated by the best Artists and Engravers, printed on toned paper in the best style.

SALMON AND FLY FISHING IS A SPECIALITY.

The Natural History of Fish and Fishing is specially dealt with, and Articles by the foremost authorities on "The Aquaria," "Gossip," and "The Clubs," are a special feature.

Reports from all the principal Rivers and Lakes in the United Kingdom by our special reporters, form a distinctive feature of "FISHING."

Mr George Kelson's Articles on Salmon Fishing, with illustrations, appear weekly.

This Journal is particularly attractive and interesting to members of Angling Clubs and Associations. Articles given, with portraits, on the History of, and facts connected with, Angling Clubs and Associations. These Articles are specially illustrated by Mr Alfred Bryan. The series include all the prominent Associations and Clubs in Great Britain and Ireland.

Notes by Mr J. P. Wheeldon appear weekly.

FISHING TACKLE, and other Requisites for Salmon and other Anglers, &c. &c., is examined, tried, and reported upon by competent judges.

Everything of interest to Anglers, Salmon and Fly Fishers, Fly Dressers, Fish Culturists, and Naturalists, finds a place in the columns of "FISHING," and is illustrated when thought desirable, especially Salmon Fishing and Salmon Flies.

CHROMO-LITHOGRAPHED PLATES, IN COLOURS, illustrating "BRITISH FISHES," are presented to Subscribers of "FISHING." The first series embrace the Freshwater Fish of Great Britain. The pictures are painted by some of our best Artists, and the plates are got up in a style worthy of the best framing.

PRIZES TO THE VALUE OF £60 will be given to the Readers of "FISHING." For full particulars see first number.

TERMS OF SUBSCRIPTION.

"FISHING" is sent direct from the Office in London, post-free, payable in advance:—For one year, 6s. 6d.; half a year, 3s. 3d.; quarter of a year, 1s. 9d. To the United States, Canada, and the Continent of Europe, and all places under Class A of Postal Union, for twelve months, 10s.

In order to preserve the Coloured Presentation Plates from damage, which would be caused by folding for post, we recommend subscribers to have the copies that contain Plates posted rolled in special prepared cases, for which the charge of 2s. per annum extra on the inland subscription and 4s. per annum on the foreign subscription is made.

WALTER BATES, Publisher, 182 Strand, London, W.C.

HORSE, CATTLE, and SHEEP MEDICINES

By Royal Appointment.

DAY, SON, & HEWITT,
Inventors and Proprietors of the Original

STOCK BREEDER'S MEDICINE CHEST,
FOR ALL DISORDERS IN HORSES, CATTLE, CALVES, SHEEP, & LAMBS.

Patronised by Royalty, and used for over 50 years by the principal Stock Breeders, Horse Proprietors, and Agriculturists of the British Empire.

Price complete, 56s. 6d. Keep good 20 years. Carriage paid to any Port or Railway Station.

The No. 2 CHEST contains the following Matchless Preparations:—

The **CHEMICAL EXTRACT**, for Strains and Sprains, Kicks, Cuts, Wounds, Bruises, Sore Udders, all External Injuries, and Ewes Lambing.

The **GASEOUS FLUID**, for Fret, Colic, or Gripes in Horses, the Scour and Debility in Cattle and Sheep.

The **RED DRENCH**, for Cleansing after Calving and Lambing, for Yellows, Fevers, Epidemics, and all Inflammatory Disorders.

The **RED PASTE BALLS**, for Coughs and Colds, Conditioning Horses, and imparting a mole-like Sleekness of Coat.

The "**BRONCHOLINE**," for Husk and Hoose in Sheep and Lambs; and the "**GASEODYNE**," "**CARMINATIVE CHALK**," "**ALCOHOLIC ETHER**," &c.

Price of Chest, complete, including "Key to Farriery," £2. 16s. 6d.

Sent Carriage paid. Each Article can be had separately in Boxes.

CAUTION.—Beware of Imitations, and see that the name of DAY, SON, & HEWITT is on all Bottles and Packets.

DAY, SON, AND HEWITT,
22 DORSET STREET, BAKER STREET, LONDON, W.; & WANTAGE, BERKS.

www.ingramcontent.com/pod-product-compliance
Lightning Source LLC
Chambersburg PA
CBHW030252170426
43202CB00009B/716